Bite-Sized Books

Stop House Prices Rising!

The Essential First Fix
For the Broken Housing Market

Conall Boyle

Steven McCabe

Cover by

Dean Stockton

Published by Bite-Sized Books Ltd 2022

Bite-Sized Books Ltd 8th Floor, 20 St. Andrews Street, London EC4A 3AY, UK

Registered in the UK. Company Registration No: 9395379

ISBN: 9781739726102

Contents

About the authors

Conall Boyle trained and worked as an engineer in Lucas Industries in Birmingham before spending many decades teaching economics and statistics to 'Built Environment' students at Birmingham City University. As well as having researched aspects of the housebuilding sector whilst working as an academic, Conall's interest in house prices has continued into retirement. Conall can be contacted through email (**conallboyle@hotmail.com**) and his regular blog can be accessed at:

http://housescheaperbettermore.blogspot.com/.

Dr Steven McCabe is Associate Professor at the Institute for Design, Economic Acceleration & Sustainability (IDEAS) and Senior Fellow within the Centre for Brexit Studies, both of which are based at Birmingham City University. Steven is a long-standing academic having taught economics and business since 1987 and writes and comments in the media extensively on management, business matters and politics.

As well as writing a number of chapters dealing with Brexit, inequality and the pandemic, Steven has co-edited *Brexit and Northern Ireland, Bordering on Confusion* (published in 2019), *English Regions After Brexit: Examining Potential Change through Devolved Power* (published in 2020), and *Exploring the Green Economy, Issues, Challenges, and Benefits* and *Green Manufacturing, what this involves and how to achieve success* both published in 2021.

Introduction

What this book seeks to achieve

There are many things wrong with housing in the UK. Houses in Britain are some of the smallest in Europe. They are poorly built and the vast majority are unable to cope well with climate change. As regular news reports suggest, new-built houses are frequently fault-ridden. Where housing is needed most, there's an inadequate supply. The great dream of a 'Home-Owning Democracy' which Prime Minister Margaret Thatcher so eulogised in the 1980s has been fading away for decades; owner-occupation reached a peak in 2003. Modestly well-off older folk live in fear that their houses may be seized to pay for their care. The young are increasingly concerned they'll never be able to afford to get on the 'housing ladder'.

There's universal agreement that the British housing market is broken and urgently needs fixing. However, while house-prices keep rising these problems will worsen. Rising prices makes almost any kind of home unaffordable, even those for those on average incomes. Older homeowners find their accumulated equity is needed to help their children buy their own home, the so called 'bank of mom and dad'. Any notion of retirement in comfort continues to be a dream. Successive governments have viewed houses as 'cash cows' and the increased equity is used for social care costs. Recent attempts to resolve the conundrum of how to pay for care has merely tinkered. Cynics suggest the political consequences of confronting rising house prices are considered too great.

That is why this book focusses on just one topic, how to stop house prices rising faster than inflation generally, and at the very least, to ensure they do not rise faster than the average income of working people. We have come to expect economic progress in that goods and services become cheaper and, mostly, better in quality and performance. Unfortunately, British housing appears to be very different. Housing, it must be acknowledged, is not a normal consumer product. It frequently appears immune from conventional rules of supply and demand in that higher prices should encourage new firms to enter the market. However, unlike most other products we purchase – food being an exception – housing requires land. Nonetheless, even with an abundance of land on which housing can be built, planning permission having been granted to developers, supply remains woefully inadequate.

The great, but now neglected, economist Galbraith puts like this, "The inadequate provision of housing at modest cost in contrast with that of say automobiles or cosmetics, can be considered the *greatest single default of modern capitalism*" (1987:290)(our emphasis). Significantly, in recent decades, at the core of what is a relentless rise in house prices is the belief by almost everyone connected with the process from developers to purchasers is that a home is an asset. Housing is something to be considered as an investment rather than its utilitarian purpose to live in and, for parents, raise families. As such, it is the UK financial system and the freedom it has been given to exploit the economics of assets, which hugely influences house prices and must be understood.

Crucially, the nature of the asset financial institutions exploit is not, or so it seems to us, widely understood. It's apparent that the financial sector freed to make virtually unlimited loans exploits the asset underlying houses. This has has resulted in a huge and erratic inflation in the prices of something we all require but must pay more and more to own, namely somewhere to live.

Only by explaining the proximate cause of the rise in house price rises can we hope to eventually rein them in. Specifically, only by stopping further damaging price rises and, ultimately, creating circumstances conducive to a gentle slide downwards, we contend, will allow the possibility of the housing market delivering high quality, reasonably priced houses in abundance. Indeed, we believe, unless the ever-increasing rise in house price is stopped, the many reforms posited by those claiming to understand British housing will have little impact. This therefore must be the overriding priority. Naturally, the vexed question is, of course, how?

Supply or Demand?

It is obvious that there many things wrong with housing in the UK, but the problem the vast majority of commentators agree on is their price. Historically, British house prices are far too high. At the time of writing, though there are warnings of a slowing due to interest rate increases combined with a 'cost of living' crisis caused by rapidly rising inflation, many believe the trajectory of British house prices will remain upwards. Taking a demand approach, this book identifies the mechanisms which continue to inflate house prices. Rather than being concerned with land and interventions intended to boost its supply, we instead address what we consider to be the initial factor which has fuelled the rise in house prices, the availability of mortgage finance. Specifically, we contend, an apparently unlimited supply of loans available to house-buyers has ensured the price of all housing in this country has risen at such an alarming rate.

But where do the lenders —mainly banks— obtain so much money to lend? Using the latest insight of what's referred to as *Modern Monetary Theory*, this well-founded but not widely understood analysis will show how banks seem to have limitless funds for lending. That leads to the first technique of stopping house prices rising—by which the supply of mortgage funds could be restrained which would reduce effective demand for housing. By pressing down on the banks' ability to lend for mortgages, demand would be constrained and the price of houses in this country be stabilised.

What makes UK financial institutions so keen to lend to buyers for house purchase? There is an asset involved. This is critical as a house provides the collateral to make mortgage lending a 'safe bet'. The value of the building, which represents a depreciating asset, accounts for a small part of the 'house' price. It is the other part of the bargain — the land that the house sits on — which provides by far the greater part of the collateral. It is the land each house stands on which mostly underpins any mortgage loan. So it is the value of the **plot,** which we'll define later, that is the main asset. This is a difficult idea for many to acknowledge even though there's a wealth of academic work underpinning this contention.

Which leads to two further methods intended to constrain house price rises. Since the rise in prices is overwhelmingly due to plot-value inflation, bearing down on land values removes part of this asset cost. Take out some, or all, of the plot value and the overall house-price will fall. We identify the two main ways this can be done, which are either to take all housing land into public ownership or to tax away the value of the plot. Though seeming drastic, this is not unprecedented. Public ownership of housing land in Singapore has produced, according to *The Economist*, the best solution worldwide to the crisis in housing markets.

The other fix, land value taxation, has near-unanimous approval from economists as an appropriate, non-distortionary form of revenue raising for governments. Its chief virtue is that it recaptures some or all of the publicly created value in the plots that houses sit on. No new ideas are involved here. Academic analysts have variously identified the mechanisms pushing up house prices and the methods that could be used to stabilise or even reduce prices paid. What is new here is that these ideas are brought together in one place, and the specific objective of stopping price rises explored.

Of course, we accept, many, perhaps the vast majority, of homeowners, potential inheritors, bankers and many politicians, particularly in the Conservative Party, *want* house prices to continue rising. The political prospects for implementing the recommendations we advocate are explored and, we argue, their prospects appear reasonably optimistic. We finish with one practical example which could commence the process of stopping house prices rising.

Conall Boyle and Dr. Steven McCabe January 2022

Chapter 1

122 years of house prices in the UK

When things are going well there's a tendency to simply ignore them. This has been especially true concerning house-prices. There's always been an abundance of records for house sales. However, it wasn't until the 1970s that such information was collated into a proper Index of house-prices. Initially, two building societies, the Halifax and the Nationwide, produced their Indexes, which proved useful to those monitoring changes. It also provides headlines for the media, who know a good story when they see one! The 1970s, it should be remembered, was a period when the price of British houses first experienced a rapid and unexpected rise. Although followed by a fall in prices, further spikes and troughs have hit the price of houses. It was not until the late 1990s that officialdom took an interest in this, with government producing its own House Price Index for the UK (UK HPI). To get data for house prices before the 1970s we have to draw on some hefty academic research.

This lack of official interest is easy to understand when we look at the graph for house prices in the UK (below) for the period 1899—2021[1]. The data on this graph show house prices in 'real' terms, that is, adjusted for inflation.

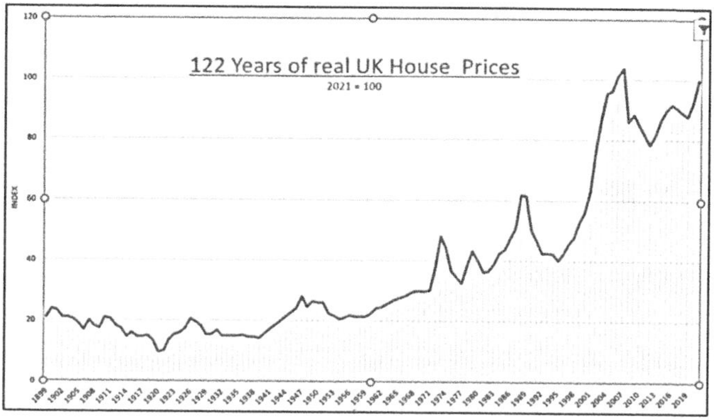

———-YEARS———-

The picture before 1970 is one of considerable stability (apart from some volatility after the World Wars). Most changes were gradual, although a general downward trend is clear before 1939. One major surprise might be to learn that houses were getting *cheaper* every year from 1925 right up until 1939. This was a 'Golden Age' for the housing market. Falling house-prices meant that more of those on average earnings could find better accommodation for

[1] The earlier data on this graph is derived from on Knoll, Katharina, Moritz Schularick, and Thomas Steger. "No Price Like Home: Global House Prices, 1870–2012." *American Economic Review* 107, no. 2 (February 2017): 331–53. https://doi.org/10.1257/aer.20150501. This was then spliced together with earlier and current data values taken from Halifax house price information.

themselves and families. The new houses — mostly of the 3-bedroomed semi type — were built in abundance. Despite what the critics said at the time, they were well-built and they still command a good price to this day.

Even after World War 2, the situation remained fairly benign. Although the trend was upwards, increases in prices were modest. The notion that buying housing represented a way to 'get rich quick' would have seemed ludicrous. Post-war rates of construction ensured an increase in the supply of houses being built, initially for the public sector, but equally by developers for private ownership. The demand for home ownership was well-served. As such, there was a steady transition from renting to home ownership.

The 1970s: a dramatic change in price movements

It's easy to see that 1972 saw the start of big change in the way house prices moved, a pattern which has continued right up to today. No more gradual trends. In what represented a shock to the housing market, prices rose rapidly then dropped back again. However, the decrease was not back to the level before the rapid rise, but somewhat higher. This was the first of the four spikes on the house price graph up to the present day (2022). Each time the pattern is the same — a steady rise up to a peak in 1979, 1989 and then an absolute humdinger in 2007 just before the Great Financial Crash. After the peak comes the trough, a partial drop back, but still higher than before. But our graph only shows *four* such spikes. It seems almost inevitable that sometime in or after 2022 there will be another *fifth* spike. When will this happen and what sort of crash will it be?

The one thing that stands out from this jagged picture is that despite the volatility, the trend is inexorably upwards. Every spike is higher than the previous one. After the spike comes the trough, but the trough never goes below the previous value. Remember that these are 'real' values adjusted for inflation. The paper values of actual money prices would make it look much, much worse.

Why the 1990s were such bad news for homeowners

A source of confusion for some, and huge distress for owners of property, is the understanding of 'real' prices. During periods such as the 1970s and 1980s, when retail inflation was high, 'real' (inflation adjusted) house-prices may have decreased in the slumps, but the actual amount of money 'on paper' that a house was worth on the market continued to rise. The period 1989-1997 was the exception. Even the paper amounts of the value of houses declined. Since the mortgage contract specifies an actual sum of money borrowed, a significant number of homeowners found themselves in what's known as 'negative equity'. In those miserable times many, especially those whose income declined because of job losses, believed their prospects of keeping up with their mortgage re-payments to be so bleak that 'they threw the towel in'. Defaults and repossessions increased significantly which, in turn, further depressed house prices.

The final peak in 2007?

The graph above shows a final peak being reached in 2007. At that point house prices, in real terms, had risen to well over three (in some case four) *times* the levels of earlier years. House prices were increasing well ahead of wages, too. Little wonder that for many, houses were regarded as a commodity well worth investing in. Moreover, the notion that any house purchased was more than just a home became embedded in collective consciousness. Interest in house prices and analysis of indices became mainstream as homeowners calculated the value of their primary asset.

This was seen most emphatically during the build-up to the GFC — the Great Financial Crash — of 2008. The usual explanation for the Crash is 'sub-prime mortgages'. These were mortgages for house purchase by borrowers whose financial circumstances were extremely risky. In the quest to create additional business, American mortgage lenders were willing to provide finance in a way that can only be described as reckless. Providing finance to those 'NINJAs' (No Income, No Job, no Assets) may have seemed quite prudent in a rising market. Any increase in the value of their home would mean that should they be forced to relinquish ownership it would be worth more than the loan.

Unfortunately, as the size of the subprime market increased, so did any risk of a fall in the market. When some of those with subprime loans defaulted, it had a knock-on effect which rapidly developed into a financial crisis of unprecedented magnitude. The financial services industry had taken advantage of widespread deregulation to create a vast network of 'derivatives' of loans that had multiplied up, 'leveraged' in the jargon, the risk involved. What had started as a small 'leak' within the American financial system, had, with alarming speed turned into global crisis which resulted in the collapse of a number of banks and other lenders and threated the very nature of capitalism.

Heading towards another peak (and crash) in 2026?

Average prices in the British housing market started decreasing in the year prior to the 2008 GFC. Subsequently, you'd imagine a somewhat chastened financial sector would have been extremely cautious in facilitating more loans in the form of mortgages. Up to a point!

Again, reading off the graph, you can see that, following an initial large drop in 2007-8, house prices continued their sinking trend until 2013. Then something surprising happened. House prices started to rise once again. Five years after the GFC, the mortgage lenders calculated that, because of QE (which had repaired their balance sheets) they possessed more than adequate reserves and started lending again. We'll explain where banks obtain the money to lend as mortgages in a later chapter. Curiously, Covid-19 has provided the latest twist in the saga of British house prices. Although the pandemic has caused a major hit to the economy, yet more money in the economy has been created by government through yet another injection of QE. The consequence is that rather than house prices falling, as most commentators had predicted, they have risen.

Our graph finishes at the end of 2021, a year in which house prices rose by 9.8 per cent (according to the Halifax). That's still more than 5 per cent when adjusted for inflation. The horrifying thing about this is that house prices have almost climbed back up to the crazy levels reached just before the 2008 GFC! This is madness, and is a clear dereliction of duty by the banking authorities and the politicians and their civil servants advising them, who are responsible for this policy. It has to be stopped before another devastating crash hits the economy, and with it the housing market.

Indeed, though many analysts suggest that in 2022, particularly if interest rates increase, there'll be a drop in the rate at which house prices increase, others suggest this relative decline will be temporary. Nonetheless, the portents are that yet another damaging surge-to-a-peak boom in house prices is occurring. Notably, 2026 has been pencilled in by maverick British housing expert, Fred Harrison, who has an impressive track record in predicting major changes to prices, as the likely date of the next bust in the housing market[1].

Summary

Endless waves of rising house prices may be a source of joy for existing homeowners, politicians, banks with money to lend, and others besides, but they create a very dismal prospect for many, especially youngsters aspiring to

---

[1] The Appendix has a list of authors and their books and papers referred to. This is also a good source for 'suggested further reading'.

become homeowners — Generation Rent as they are called. As we've shown, this is a relatively new phenomenon. Before the 1970s, house prices rose slowly and steadily and even, in the 1930s, managed a sustained and gentle fall. If, following Covid19, another steep rise in house prices is permitted, this is bad news for British society and should be stopped. This book will explain in detail how price rises can be stopped.

But why so timid? Shouldn't we be looking to bring house-prices *down,* down to the much more affordable levels of the 1960s? Moreover, if we are really serious, then why should house prices not be at the 1930s levels, when prices were *one-fifth* of what they are today and pretty much the same in all parts of the UK? Eventually, yes. Unfortunately, so broken and distorted is our present housing market that any change must be brought in gradually. Many homeowners have secured huge mortgages. Any sudden and rapid decline in housing market would engender appalling misery. So for now the aim is to **stop** the seemingly unstoppable rise in house prices.

Chapter 2

A broken housing market—the result of spiralling prices.

When house prices remained fairly steady, before 1970, the market worked well, producing a steady supply of new houses at prices aspiring homeowners could afford. Existing houses were equally inexpensive and, though considered by many to have been built to superior standards and more spacious when compared to their more recent alternatives, could also be draughty and harder to keep warm. Importantly, those aspiring to become homeowners, primarily the young, were easily able to fulfil this objective.

Fast forward to the 21st century and a very different picture emerges. Homeownership reached a peak in 2003 and has been steadily declining since. Un-affordability as measured by price-to-income ratios has soared. The rate of housebuilding has been, at best, inadequate. As regular reporting of dissatisfaction among some purchasers of new housing shows, the product frequently fails to achieve standards expected.

If you want to know more about the UK's 'Broken Housing Market' in full and depressing detail, there have been some excellent books on the subject published in the last few years. Usefully, there's is a wealth of up-to-date information in all of these well-researched books. If you want to know more detail about what's wrong, these are the books to go for, and the people to listen to. Helpfully, and entertainingly, YouTube contains a wealth of talks and lectures by the authors we've cited. Just search under their names together with 'housing market'.

A list of these books and brief notes on their contents is given as an addendum to this chapter. Because our main purpose here is to describe the *solutions* which will fix the broken housing market, we'll just go briefly over the features that make the problem so bad. Good though these books are, the 'solutions' section is usually just one chapter at the end, often a rag-bag of good ideas, but not enough in themselves to fix the housing market. This is a solutions book, so our aim is not to dwell on the problems but to tell you what's needed to fix it, in full.

Politics, more particularly the willingness by politicians to 'do something' that sounds as if they care, is a major contributory factor in making the housing market worse. Failing to do what it takes to *really* fix the housing market is usually a result of cowardice. After all politicians want to get re-elected. However, before implementing a solution to the problem that is likely to be successful, let's review the main symptoms of Britain's 'broken' housing market.

The symptoms of the Britain's 'broken' housing market

Rates of homeownership falling

Homeownership steadily climbed in the 1980s following Mrs Thatcher's exhortation that citizens should be willing to become part of the home owning democracy.

Interestingly, this expression dates to 1923 when first used by a Conservative MP, Noel Skelton, when he wrote a series of short articles for *The Spectator,* subsequently combined into a pamphlet for his party, *Constructive Conservatism.* Whilst there was a slight dip in the percentage of owner-occupiers, with and without a mortgage, in the early 1990s, a mini peak of 68.5% was reached in 1994. Thereafter it remained flat for about three years.

After 1997 'things could only get better' under Prime Minister Blair. Home ownership advanced once again and to all all-time high of 71% in 2003. However, as prices of housing rapidly increased in the run-up to the GFC the proportion of those owning their own homes declined. The latest available statistics published by the government show that 63% of households owned their homes, with or without a mortgage. Though this varies across the UK regions and ethnic groups, younger people are far less likely to own their homes.

This inter-generational inequality would be even worse were it not for the Bank of Mum and Dad — the parents helping their children get on the housing ladder. According to a survey by Zoopla in 2020, nearly two-thirds of parents (64%) whose grown-up children own homes said they helped with the deposit. Their average contribution came in at a massive £32,440[1].

[1] Giving away a large sum of money, even to your own children, has been a strange experience for one of us! A solicitor has to attest that the money is (a) yours, not criminally laundered, and that (b) it is a gift, not a loan.

Despite the promises of the Johnson government, this age difference is highly likely to increase, if house prices continue to rise. As many commentators point out, though those with parents who own their own houses will, through inheritance, provide them with a potential ability to purchase their own homes, this is hardly ideal. Because we're living longer, this will merely ensure the age profile continues to be skewed towards the old. Moreover, social care costs will, for those unable to look after themselves, reduce the money available. An even greater worry is that as the proportion of those who cannot afford to purchase their own homes for the entirety of their working lives increases, their ability to fund rents – which are continuing to rise – from meagre pension income will develop into a crisis. A drastic reduction in the availability of good quality and affordable social housing further exacerbates this crisis.

Size of houses

Britain's housing stock, on average, contains the second smallest houses in Europe. As the pandemic has proven, particularly for the many who work from home, that there is too little space within their property as well as its environs. This is seen as fundamental to the physical and mental health of the inhabitants. As well as being too small, British houses are cold and draughty, compared to other European countries. Retro-fitting insulation, updating boilers and so on may go some way to rectifying this, but eventually maybe it would be better knock down the whole house and replace it with something much better.

In the new-build sector it is plain to see that as the price of development land has massively increased, the size of plots and the houses/gardens built have shrunk as developers try to make what they regard as an adequate return on investment. Critics would say that builders are making profits and ensuring the companies' wealth at the expensive of tiny houses for the customer.

Unaffordability

One of the frequently cited measures used by analysts to assess the state of housing is to compare average prices for housing to earnings. This produces a single nationwide 'affordability' ratio. This will vary considerably due to localised circumstances and conditions, but it provides a graphic 'state of play'. Here's what it looked like over the last 174 years.

1

This is a story of steady progress in Victorian times followed by odd developments during and after the two world wars. Ignore the strange spike downwards during and after WW1, and the post-war spike upwards in the 1940s. On this graph it's the 1920s and 30s that stand out as a golden era for home-buyers and owners. By the end of the 1930s of the average-priced house was less than *four* times the average salary. Of course averages are always somewhat dangerous as a measure as they don't adequately present the full range of data.

Throughout the 1950s and 1960s affordability remained relatively stable. Rising wages and a steady supply of new housing stock, especially after the second world war, enabled access to those seeking better quality accommodation. However, as shown above, following the boom, then crash, for house prices in the mid-1970s as described in the previous chapter, any return to a reasonable four-to-one ratio of affordability ratio is fleeting at best. The trend in the ratio is ever upwards, and now stands at more than *eight* times average wages.

This final build-up prior to the 2008 GFC now seems to be baked in. The mini-slump that followed the crash was soon followed by a rise, so that affordability is at the worst it's been for more than a century. Because wage growth has not kept pace with house prices, it's very likely we could see the issue of affordability grow larger.

Rental sector unsatisfactory

Because so many, especially young potential first-time buyers, have been effectively priced out of being able to achieve ownership, they are forced to rent instead. A cynical interpretation is that insecure conditions for renters were deliberately engineered to make landlordism more attractive. Houses that might have added to owner-occupation have been purchased by landlords to for rental income in the 'buy-to-let' boom. Home-owners who need to move elsewhere are holding on to their old houses and renting them out. The dire conditions of many of those who are forced to rent has been memorably described by Chloe Timperley in her 2020 *Generation Rent Why you can't buy a home (or even rent a good one)*. In theory choosing to rent or to buy a home should be a neutral choice depending on circumstances. In Germany a tightly regulated rental market is thriving and seen as a natural state of affairs. It is our own self-imposed tragedy that the rental sector treats its tenants so badly.

The government's 2017 response

The broken market could be fixed if only we could increase the supply of new-built houses, seems to be the economists' free-market-driven idea behind the government paper *Fixing Our Broken Housing Market*. This is standard fare trotted out by many 'sensible' commentators. So too says the Government, apparently. If only the developers would build lots more houses, that would fix it. As you might expect in an official Report, they do not blame Government! No, others are responsible for not producing vastly more houses. Here's how they explain it:

"The problem [of under-supply] is threefold: not enough local authorities planning for the homes they need; house building that is simply too slow; and a construction industry that is too reliant on a small number of big players." (p9)

So, it's local authorities that are unwilling to do enough! Totally ignored in this report is the idea that, maybe, the government's own legislation might be a cause.

Equally the way tax is inflicted on the housing market is not considered. Nor do they face the fact that bailing out of banks means they have virtually unlimited funds for mortgages. Each of these on their own are significance but combined they undoubtedly contributed to the latest house price bubble.

So how can we be so sure that increasing the supply by building more houses won't bring down prices? Perhaps the recent experience in Spain and Ireland should give us 'food for thought'. House-building booms occurred in both these countries prior to the 2008 crash. However, this did not bring down prices. Instead, both experienced what are referred to as 'ghost estates' consisting of half-built stock strewn across the countryside. As demand has returned some of these are now complete though many were simply demolished. Housing as we shall see is not a normal product in a normal market, so the standard economic calculations won't work. Of course in the long run many more homes should be built, but until what is broken in the housing market is fixed building more will have little effect on holding back prices rises.

Another government paper *Analysis of the determinants of house price changes (2018 ad hoc publication)* concludes, based on a theoretical model that "If housing stock increases by 1 per cent, house prices would fall by around 2 per cent." There are 28 million homes in the UK housing stock (2021) and house prices rose by 10% (5% in real terms) in 2021. Just to stop that 5% real rise in prices would require the building of 700,000 *additional* dwellings according to the 'rule-of-thumb' given above. Government statistics show that around 120,000 new dwellings were completed in each of the last few years. So what magic mechanism will multiply production up *six-fold*? This is the clearest evidence why we say that the economists favourite nostrum of 'build-more' is nonsense. It is wildly unrealistic for now in today's broken market.

Government claims lack of supply is to blame. So what do they do? Boost Demand of course!

Schemes like 'help to buy', stamp duty 'holidays' as well as deposit insurance have been introduced with the avowed intention of helping youngsters get on the housing ladder. The effect on prices has been uniformly one-sided. It has added additional fuel to the demand side of the market. The result, unsurprisingly, is that prices were pushed up even higher. Far from helping the aspirations of those wanting to buy their first house becomes it makes it even more difficult.

A very good piece of research on the effect of a 'stamp duty holiday' shows this to be so. Anne Bolster, was tasked with 'Evaluating the impact of stamp duty land tax of first time buyer's relief'. What she discovered, in a very intelligent analysis of a stamp duty 'holiday' in 2010-12, when first-time buyers (FTBs) were exempted on purchases up to £250,000, was devastating. The result of the 'holiday' was that, at most, only 2% more FTBs were coaxed onto the market.

Notably, transactions hardly increased. Bolster recons that it cost the Government £160,000 for each additional FTB. Worse, government intervention meant prices paid by all purchasers, including the FTBs, increased. Sellers benefitted by pocketing most of the increase though, if they were moving upwards in the chain, would have to pay more for their next home. So, Bolster estimated, the Cameron/Clegg coalition government wasted at least £300 million of tax revenue while failing to help FTBs.

Here's what the House of Lords Built Environment Committee reported[1] on 10th January 2022 on Help to Buy: "We find that the Government's Help to Buy scheme, which will have cost around £29 billion in cash terms by 2023, inflates prices by more than its subsidy value in areas where it is needed the most." What stupidity! What waste! This is 'help' the first time buyers can do without.

Summary - supply or demand?

You can't buck the market. Increasing supply is always a good way to reduce price paid in any normal market, isn't it? So why won't the constant calls to build more houses, even if heeded, result in more affordable homes? The reality is the housing market does not operate in the same way as for the vast majority of other commodities. The decision to buy is frequently driven by a desire not to miss out in a rising market.

When it comes to house-prices, economists seem stumped. If there was a conventional economic policy which produced cheaper and better houses, surely it would have been applied already? Considerable suffering and

---

[1] HL Paper 132 *Meeting housing Demand* House of Lords Built Environment Committee 1st Report of Session 2021–22 published 10 January 2022

disappointment by FTBs would have been saved as a result? Housing in Britain needs fixing. Unfortunately, however, the government's actions suggest they have no real intention of bringing down house-prices. So, arguing that building more homes will fix it is a just a way of distracting attention away from the real solution.

Critically, there *is* an economic answer to this puzzle, but it requires stepping outside the dominant neo-classical model which is prevalent in our universities and administrators. The first obvious question to ask about the never-ending price rises is, what's driving them up? What is the influence pumping up house prices faster than inflation? To provide an answer we need to look at the banking system and the newly emerging economic consensus as to the way in which the money we use is brought into being. However, before doing this, we'd like to put in a good word for, arguably, the organisations most criticised for the crisis caused by house price increases, namely the housebuilders. They were among our students when we taught on relevant courses and, in the mid-1980s, one of the authors of this book worked for a major housebuilder.

ADDENDUM to Chapter 2

Some writers and commentators who know what they're talking about when describing the broken housing market, and also give a suggestions about fixing it.

Danny Dorling is a prolific and widely respected author on various social problems of our times. In 2015 he wrote an exhaustive examination of the British housing market, *All that is Solid: How the Great Housing Disaster*

Defines our times, and what to do about it. This book is a treasure trove of facts and graphs illustrating how bad things are. Unfortunately, his 'what to do about it' chapter, though containing an abundance of sensibly considered ideas, doesn't produce the 'killer punch', the solution that will really fix the broken market for housing.

Perhaps the most analytical and research-based book on British housing is written by a trio of academics, **Josh Ryan-Collins, Toby Lloyd & Laurie MacFarlane** and published in 2017, *Re-thinking the economics of Land and Housing.* This book presents three fixes that form the basis for this book. One fix is for the government to take more control over bank lending for mortgages. Alternatively, if all of the land that houses are built be taken into public ownership, in effect, nationalised that would do the trick. Less drastically, though controversially, they recommend the value of all housebuilding plots should be taxed away. We've based the solutions in this book on these three 'fixes'.

One of the authors, **Josh Ryan-Collins**, subsequently produced a shorter, 'popular' version of this book in 2019, *Why Can't you afford a home?* in which he emphasises his contention that most commentators have based their views on how to fix the housing market on the wrong assumption. Specifically, Ryan-Collins asserts, measures to boost the *supply* of housing will not succeed until the financial forces driving *demand* for housing are controlled. As such, his thesis is very similar to this book. However, unlike the trio of academic authors, we'll explain in a straightforward way what they are all about and why this can achieve the objective of fixing the broken British housing market.

Liam Halligan, a right-wing journalist who writes for the *Telegraph,* knows the housebuilding industry well and is respected by many within the sector. As a consequence, his 2021 book, *Home Truths: The UK's chronic housing shortage – How it happened, why it matters and how to solve it,* represents is an extremely important contribution from outside academe. Halligan forensically assesses the reasons he believes there is a crisis of the British housing market and what he thinks is needed to address the underlying problems he identifies. Crucially, though he makes some policy suggestions aimed at fixing the supply side of the housing market, he rejects the demand-side fixes described above. It's possible Halligan is treading carefully lest he upset his Telegraph-reading audience.

Chapter 3

Housebuilders not to blame, although they could do better

It's easy to blame housebuilders for the broken state of the housing market. They're on the frontline and taking decisions about what to charge those who purchase their product. Though in the past they have experienced tough times, in recent years there are many stories of major housebuilders making record fortunes. Media coverage tends to be less than effusive in their support for the handful of large companies which effectively control the majority of new houses now built in this country. They criticise both the bosses' huge pay-packets, and the fault-ridden nature of many new homes.

Specifically, companies engaged in housebuilding are repeatedly singled out and blamed for the apparently poor quality, lack of design features and, most of all, not building enough of their products. They're equally condemned for hoarding vast tracts of land which, having been granted planning permission for housebuilding, could immediately be developed. With prices so high, it's argued by critics, surely housebuilders have every incentive build more houses? After all, it may be assumed, this will increase profits

But it's back to the house-price graphs again. Since 1970 this has been a jagged 'see-saw' In the 1970s a crash in house prices meant large housebuilding developments were put on hold or abandoned at short notice. As well as the fact that many sites consisted of partly constructed houses, bankruptcy was common among many whose capital was invested in purchasing the land and buying materials. Housebuilders learned from this experience and are now more rational in adopting a cautious approach.

This may be explained by what many see as the malign power of large developers who have the will, and deep pockets, to outbid smaller regional and local counterparts. Cash-flow is essential to all businesses but those large house-builders that have survived have energetically engaged in both debt- and operating-cost reduction. Large builders have become efficient in ensuring they can manipulate the market to suit their needs. They buy land when the economy is in the doldrums and can afford to sit on their 'land bank' until the time is right to sell when the environment is more benign. Incentives offered by government, such as 'Help to Buy' and the Stamp Duty 'holiday' have, according to research carried out by Sheffield Hallam University, enabled large house-builders to enjoy profits of up to 500% and, in the case of Persimmon, the UK's largest provider, to make £66,000 profit on every house and its directors to share a £400 million bonus. Higher costs are passed onto potential customers who, faced with a lack of supply, must pay more for the new houses which are generally smaller than those built a generation ago. This is good for developers and, as cynics contend, where is their incentive to increase the supply of new houses?

This explains one of the characteristics of contemporary housebuilders, the strategy of waiting for a spell of rising house-prices, then 'drip-feeding' their product onto the market. Another factor is that they are selling into a local market. A sudden rush of an estate of hundreds of new houses would have a depressing effect on the local market, which would not be a sensible business tactic. This allows housebuilders to test the market and adjust prices according to demand. There's also an incentive for purchasers to buy early as prices tend to rise as the development progresses.

Another feature of the housing market is that the buying public, demand in the jargon, see new and old houses as inter-changeable. Indeed, surveys show that buyers often *prefer* older houses. This is because older houses tend to be better built and have more space. If they lack modern amenities or facilities, this can be remedied by refurbishment. Since the vast majority of houses on the market are second-hand (about 80% according to Land Registry sales data), they set the overall price. New-build producers therefore become 'price-followers'.

There are very few products where new and 'pre-used' are considered to be equally desirable. We might blame the housebuilders for producing such uninspiring homes. One peculiar feature is the lack of branding. Once a house has been built and sold, you'll find no sign to indicate the name of the firm which built it. For-sale advertisements for second-hand homes rarely, if ever, state 'Persimmon' or 'Charles Church' or whoever, though we are aware that when the houses of one now defunct midlands-based housebuilder went on the market owners referred to the original builder which had gained a reputation for quality. Nonetheless, we note, among housebuilders there is remarkably little differentiation or, it must be stressed, evidence of innovation. British housebuilders are nothing if not conservative in their approach to selling a product which, beyond some aesthetic flourishes, is remarkably similar.

Inefficient builders pushing up prices?

Much emphasis is placed on academic research that the construction industry exhibits poor labour productivity. Reports produced invariably recommend more training of skilled workers needs to be undertaken. So, it may be asked, does the fact that houses produced using standard components and materials, built in traditional ways by poorly trained operatives, lead to higher prices? According to the statistics produced by the Building Cost Information Service, the cost per square metre of construction (adjusted for inflation), has not significantly increased in the last few decades. For some parts of the construction there appears to be little technical development. Bricklayers have been laying clay bricks on top of each other with mortar for centuries.

However, those manufacturing products which are supplied to the housebuilders have invested in innovation and many cost-saving developments have taken place. For example, guttering and pipes for rainwater and domestic waste to sewers is no longer made of heavy cast iron. Instead, much cheaper, lighter and easier-to-fit, lighter plastic components has replaced it. A modern brickworks is an amazing site with a handful workers operating fully automatic machinery producing millions of bricks phenomenally cheaply.

The good news is that the price of building (adjusted for inflation) has *not increased* over the years. But the bad news is that unlike, say, cars, TVs or computers it hasn't dropped either, but that's a story for another time. So today's housebuilders are doing the best they can. They have been helped by manufacturers outside their industry to keep costs from rising. It is market conditions which force them to operate in such an inefficient, timid way. But given the right conditions these dedicated hard-working builders, out in all weather conditions, working on muddy locations will be able to build better, faster, cheaper and in abundance, producing houses we'll all love and desire *once we fix the broken housing market.*

Chapter 4

Effective Demand fed by Finance

It's the financial sector that provides the mortgages so that buyers can pay the price

While most commentators concentrate on means of increasing the supply of houses, there's less attention paid to where the demand is coming from. It is not enough, in a market, to say that you have a need for housing. You may have a growing family to house, and an overwhelming *need* to find somewhere for them to live. You may *want* to move to a bigger house because working from home is impossible because your tiny starter home lacks space. Now that you've got on in your job you might *like* the idea of a second home by the sea.

As economists point out, needs, wants or likes are not what makes for 'effective demand'. Only by having enough money can you start demanding. However, as we know, our financial system for all but rare exceptions, works on the basis of credit; buy now pay later. This is especially true for high price items which includes housing. Very few people have the sort of liquid finance, cash, readily available to purchase a house without borrowing using what's known as a mortgage[1].

Note the special name used exclusively for a loan used buy property. A 'mortgage', derived from the French 'grip of death', uses the value of the property as security for the loan, the fancy word for this being 'collateral'. As adverts for mortgage lending typically warn, "Your home is at risk of re-possession if you do not keep up with your mortgage payments". From a lender's point of view a mortgage is a safe bet. Even if the borrowing homeowner fails to keep up the payments, there is always an asset to seize and re-sell. The lenders' only risk is if a buyer purchases at the height of a boom and, as a consequence of recession, house prices drop and there's insufficient equity to repay the loan in full.

House prices do fall. Since the whole point of this book is intended to explain how house-price stability can be engineered, lenders would be horrified if this did indeed occur, and led to house prices decreasing. Equity, the difference between what is owed on the debt, and the market price, is the value which makes the lending such a safe bet would then start to wither away. Good news for new buyers, but most un-welcome news for lenders. One way of keeping prices rising is to extend eligibility for mortgages. This is achieved by offering loans that are as close to 100% of the collateral as possible. In these circumstances the

---

[1] Usually taking the form of a legal arrangement by which a borrower obtains funds from a bank or building society and on which interest is paid in exchange for title deed of the debtor's property which, on fully payment of the debt is returned to them (known as conveyance).

supply of funds for mortgages is all-important. The availability of money to lend on mortgages is a crucial factor in supporting the effective demand by home-buyers. Where bank and building society[1] lending leads, prices follow.

The economist Steve Keen has shown there's a clear and tight correlation between new debt (bank lending) and changes in house prices. Keen has laboured for years to get main-stream economists to recognise the importance of money and banking in their analysis. He foresaw the 2008 financial crash well before it happened because he looked, unlike mainstream economists who ignore money, and at the connection between banking and debt. Since around 80% of all retail lending is for mortgages, its effect on the housing market is the dominant reason why the housing market now spikes and then sinks from time to time. Let us follow the last 50 years of financial deregulation and see what effect it had on house prices.

Chicken or egg?

There is a counter-argument that perhaps the banks and building societies only increased their lending as a response to higher house-prices. By doing so, banks would be keen to point out their obligation to society to organise the funds to keep the market functioning. But following the

---

[1] Prior to 1970 it was Building Societies, a somewhat different financial beast to Banks who issued nearly all the mortgages. After that, banks muscled in on the mortgage business, and many building societies became banks. This has significant ramifications on the availability of mortgage funds and the effect on house price rises. More about this later.

ups and downs of mortgage lending, and how this relates to bursts of financial de-regulation, tells a different story.

Reading the history of house-price peaks after each stage of banking liberalisation

Each peak and trough of the house-price graph (see Chapter 1) seems to follow uncannily from the bursts of liberalisation and de-regulation of the financial sector. From the 1970s onwards there have been four clear peaks each followed by a downward trough. Each has followed on from deliberate government policy which 'liberated' banks to lend more freely.

The first peak came in the early 1970s. The Heath government went on a 'Dash for Growth', relaxing the rules on lending and allowing other so-called secondary banks in on the game. These were smaller financial organisations many of whom organised hire purchase agreements. The main clearing banks did not engage in mortgage lending in those days, so it was these secondary banks that piled in to plug the gap left by the much more restrictive Building Societies. Of course they over-lent and, as a consequence, the financial sector imploded. The Bank of England launched a 'lifeboat' to underpin the system and financial institutions were saved.

The second spike was less prominent. In the later 1970s, the Wilson/Callaghan Labour government experienced major economic crises including devaluation and intense industrial disputes leading to the 1978-79 'winter of discontent'. Thereafter, a brief period in house price growth occurred as a result of some Keynesian stimulation, but was quickly extinguished because of Margaret Thatcher's monetarist inclination.

The third spike took longer to build up. The monetarist experiment was an attempt to control the supply of money supply by raising interest rates. Bank rates reached a high as 17% in November 1979, and mortgage repayments followed them up. In the UK most mortgages are on variable rates, meaning the lenders could do this. So mortgage repayments rose and demand for new mortgages fell. We have memories of some with large mortgages in the early-1980s being frantic with worry about how to afford the payments. Fear of losing one's home is undoubtedly powerful.

Yes, unbelievably for today's generation of younger house buyers who are used to interest rates below 6% (and sub one per cent since the GFC), interest rates on mortgages, which had been in double digits for much of the 1970s, went as high as 17% and remained above 10% until November 1984. This has the effect of dampening enthusiasm for house-purchase, and with it, house prices. However, as economic stability returned, so did confidence in house prices. A large influence in the return of confidence was de-regulation of London's financial institutions and markets, the so called 'Big Bang', in late October 1986. One major effect was that now all of the clearing banks got in on the mortgage business. Why they had held off until now is a curious story of covert regulation, nods and winks in the City and a bizarrely-named control known as The Corset. More of this in a later chapter.

This was the trigger for the *third* spike in the graph. The changes, introduced under Margaret Thatcher's second term as PM, were intended to make London preeminent as the world's most important financial centre. It allowed greater freedom for financial institutions in their ability to operate and expand business. This enabled them to increase lending. As inflation started to increase again, investment in assets became a means of hedging, protecting yourself against increased prices. Rising house prices, which coincided with falling interest rates in the mid-1980s, meant that house ownership turned out to be an excellent means of hedging.

Since banks now joined with the building societies and became freer to lend, the ability to buy became possible for those with a less than an ideal credit record to borrow. Rules on maximum size of loans were eased, and 'red-lining' was banned. This was the arrangement between lenders not to advance mortgages in unsavoury areas, which were red-lined, effectively treated as 'no go' zones on maps of areas as far as lending was concerned. 'Big Bang' assisted in creating a culture in which, if you wanted it, you could secure borrowing to have it. It should therefore come as no surprise that house prices rose rapidly and peaked in 1989. Not for the first, and certainly not the last, house prices demonstrated that what goes up will, eventually, come down.

A conjunction of economic events led to 'Black Wednesday', 16th September 1992, when there was a spectacular collapse in the value of the pound, despite John Major's Conservative government spending £3.14 billion in an attempt to prop it up. This had been necessary to ensure the pound maintained a minimum value that had been specified by the European Exchange Rate Mechanism (ERM) of which the UK was a member. Within nine and half hours, the government, which could then set the base rate, increased the prevailing interest rise from 10% to 12%, then 15% before abandoning intervention whereby the rate returned to 10%.

Black Wednesday had a devastating effect on the housing market. Economic confidence experienced a severe blow, spending was cut back and, as a consequence, unemployment rose. Because of mortgage defaults, repossessions massively increased. Britain's housing market was plunged into deep depression. Distress sales of houses at knock-down prices took the market down further. Mortgage lenders took fright and pulled back from lending on shrinking collateral. Perhaps worst of all was that slowing inflation no longer covered up falling real house prices. For many years thereafter, the price you could expect when selling a house was the same *or less* in actual money terms than what it cost. This had a deeply negative psychological effect on homeowners.

And so on to the *fourth* (and final?) spike in the house price graph. Mrs Thatcher's vision of a home-owning democracy didn't look so rosy after this. But, as always with housing, things started to perk up again. Tony Blair's Labour government had decided that only a 'Son-of Thatcher' agenda would ensure they were elected. Thus, deregulation and liberalisation continued apace. So too, inevitably, did the onward and upward pace of house-price rises. Although the period 1997-2007 has been labelled 'The

Great Moderation' by central bankers like Alan Greenspan, the financial engineering it engendered was anything but.

Lending on the security of a house (collateral) was once again seen to be a safe bet. The default rate by homeowners was very low, so the time had come to test how far it was safe to go, lending to high credit-risk homebuyers. The answer was 'quite a lot'. It seemed quite safe when all kinds of exotic financial packages which leveraged up the risk of mortgages were engineered and sold to all the major banks world-wide.

Meanwhile, house prices climbed ever upwards, seemingly proving that the risk of collateralised lending on house purchase was minimal. Because of all the leveraging, it only took a small fraction of defaulting home buyers to bring the scheme crashing down and rendering the entire banking system bankrupt. House prices peaked in 2007. It's as if the lenders had got wind of the coming GFC, which took another year to happen.

Although the rotten structures of collateralised debt based on mortgages to NINJAs — no income, no job, no asset borrowers, should have resulted in all-round bankruptcy of the banks, that's not what happened. The Central Banks of the world — the Bank of England, the Fed in America, even the EU Central bank rallied round. By Quantitative Easing which was a massive issue of credit they 'repaired the balance sheets' of the commercial banks. This as we shall see had consequences.

The housing market did drop back quite sharply after 2008, but soon steadied. By 2012 the market started rising again. A recent surge during the Covid-19 pandemic, when prices had been expected to fall, means that average real house prices in early 2022 are now almost back up to their 2008 peak. Why is this happening all over again? Why wasn't the 2008 Great Financial Crash the endpoint of this crazy spiral upwards in house prices?

Conclusion

It goes back to the banking system. Despite their record of 'incontinent' lending to hugely questionable borrowers, banks were rescued and bailed out with huge amounts of taxpayers' money, known as 'quantitative easing'. Interest rates have declined to historically, indeed extreme emergency low levels of almost zero. Chastened slightly, and with advice ringing in their ears from the Bank Regulators, mortgage lending was reined in for a while. It's back to business-as-usual now, even though the 'emergency' low-interest regime in still in place, and the pandemic has merely only reinforced it.

What this brief history demonstrates is that house price peaks almost invariably follow on from bank de-regulation and liberalisation. Let the banks rip, and they will naturally lend more for house purchase. Apart from the 2008 great financial crash, this has been quite prudent strategy for them, lending on the strength of an asset which can be relied upon. The banks have discovered just how much value can be extracted from housing, how much they can safely lend to maximise their profits.

Chapter 5

Banks can create as much money as they like, if they can find borrowers, who are mostly mortgagees

"There's no more money" claimed the writer of a handwritten note left by an outgoing Labour Treasury minister, MP for Birmingham Hodge Hill, Liam Byrne, in 2010. This, of course, was in the aftermath of the financial crash of 2008. Presumably Byrne was aware of the phenomenal amount of government money used for quantitative easing which had been used in the main to rescue the banks and create financial stability. During the Covid19 pandemic, we've seen the government dedicating vast sums of money to pay millions of workers to stay at home (furlough) as well as for track and trace and the herculean task of vaccinating – currently three times – every adult member of the population.

As many ask, where did the hundreds of billions, stated on the government's own website [1], dated 7th December 2021, to range from about £315 to £410 billion [...] the equivalent of about £4,700 to £6,100 per person in the UK", come from? Yes, it seems like there is a 'Magic Money Tree' which, usefully, has the same first letters.

---

[1] https://commonslibrary.parliament.uk/research-briefings/cbp-9309/

MMT, as a theory though regarded as recent, has been around for over a century through developing the work of economist Georg Friedrich Knapp who, in 1905, published *State Theory of Money*.

Modern Monetary Theory is the formal meaning for MMT

Before the 1970s, only building societies, needing to comply with stringent rules, would provide mortgages. They could only lend what they held in their reserves. In effect the total amount lent should be no more than what was on deposit by savers. In those days, it was necessary to practically beg for a mortgage. It wasn't enough that your salary was deemed large enough. A mortgage could be no greater than two-and-a-half times the male's salary (plus half of his wife's) and this was considered generous! Saving for the deposit had to be with the building society providing the mortgage. As a matter of prudence, mortgages were limited to a maximum percentage of the property's price. Great disappointment would be experienced if the building society's valuer decreed that you were paying too high a price. This meant that a borrower's deposit had to be larger because the maximum mortgage was reduced. Tough, buyers had to wait, comply with onerous conditions, but at least prices were held stable.

A major shift in provision of mortgages occurred in the 1970s when secondary banks entered the market. In the period 1977 to 1987, the share of mortgages provided by building societies fell from 96% to 66%. Mortgages provided by all the banks in the same period increased from 3% to 36%. The reason for this was that banks were not bound by the same rules as building societies. Whereas building societies could only lend money held through deposits, banks have always been free to be more adventurous. In the standard textbook description, banks are allowed to lend many multiples of the money they hold in reserve. Deposit £100 in a bank and they are able to lend £1,000, ten times the reserve amount. This is called 'fractional reserve banking', and as liberalisation of financial services progressed, ratios of 30 or even 50 times became commonplace and deemed perfectly prudent.

Building societies, unsurprisingly, considered themselves disadvantaged. Rather than remain mutual, owned by members, and encouraged by further de-regulation, many became banks requiring them to buy out the members. The consequence was the mortgage market became much more competitive as all those offering mortgages sought to expand their business. Frequently, introductory offers were used to attract customers wishing to obtain a mortgage. Critically, out went onerous conditions, maximum percentage mortgages, and the need to wait months before funds were made available.

In reality, rules imposed on building societies had been too stringent. Defaulting on mortgages, leading to re-possession, was very unusual. The mortgage lenders were, it's accepted, overly cautious and avoided risk. As critics of the rules asserted, building societies could lend far more with little additional risk. Avoidance of risk is considered anathema to profit-maximising capitalists. The ability to make more money by expanded lending was too good to miss. However, beneficial though this may have been to customers wishing to secure mortgages in the 1970s, it's a case of a good news story being superseded by another which, because of banks' ability to lend *unlimited* amounts of money, has had other unintended though, arguably, foreseeable, negative consequences. Welcome to the world of Modern Monetary Theory in which all that is needed is borrowers willing to invest in property. As Ann Petifor, writing in *Prospect* in July 2021 explained:

> *When banks make loans, they have always acted as "magic money trees," creating new deposits in the accounts of those who borrow from them—in effect new money.*

Brief review of Modern Monetary Theory.

It is now widely accepted by many economists, including the Bank of England, as well as enlightened journalists such as Martin Wolf of the *Financial Times,* that banks creates the overwhelming majority of our money, over 97%. When a customer is granted a loan, new money is created which will be repaid with interest. There's no limit to the amount of money in the form of credit that a bank can create. The only constraint is the supply of willing borrowers.

How did the banks acquire this astonishing privilege? That has evolved, building up over the centuries and is now seen as 'normal'. Great care has been taken not to reveal this in standard economics textbooks. Economists may describe patient lenders with money in their accounts as a necessary counterpart to the eager borrowers as the basis for lending, including, of course, mortgage lending, but bankers know what's really going on.

Where there is a sovereign currency, such as the pound sterling, there can be some degree of control over the banks exercised by the central bank (Bank of England). Ultimately, the whole currency and banking system is underpinned by the state, which is what it means to have a sovereign currency. Control can be stiffer or looser depending on the prevailing political climate. Banks are well aware they depend on the State as the lender of last resort when things go wrong such as a financial crisis.

Summary

It's the ability given to banks, and other financial intermediaries, to create unlimited amounts of loanable funds such as mortgages that has powered the unrelenting rise in house prices. Banks are happy to make most (80%), of their created money available for mortgages because of the collateral which underpins it. They have recognised that a house has a reliable asset-value far beyond its value as a product. Even Goldman Sachs admit that it's bank lending that's pushing up house prices. In a highly revealing article in the Mail on Sunday (8 Aug 2021), because banks are 'suffering' post-2008 restrictions on lending to the casino-activities, they are forced to turn to mortgage lending. Competition between banks has led phenomenally low interest rates (there's a quote of five year offer from RBS fixed at 1.03%, and a two-year fix at 0.83% from Halifax). Of course, this wasn't a plea from Goldman Sachs to rein in property prices or restore sanity to the housing market. No, it was special pleading that banks should no longer be repressed. Rather, they argue, they should, once again be allowed to create the derivatives which widely existed before market suffered the calamitous crash in 2008 as a consequence of what many contend was reckless lending.

Chapter 6

One Obvious Fix: limit the money available for mortgages.

Try direct control: tell the banks to back-peddle on mortgages

Appeal to their better nature? Surprisingly, this has been tried in Ireland. The Central bank issued guidelines[1] in 2015 advising maximum loan-to-income and loan-to-value for mortgages. It seems to have been of little benefit. House prices have continued to roar away. It is easy to see why. The rules were drafted in the loosest possible way. Banks, hungry profit-seeking operators that they are, stretched them to the limit. The honesty of borrowers in reporting income was also difficult to police.

Could they have tried harder? It would be hugely disruptive to return to the pre-1970s 'gentleman's agreement' (it was sometimes called 'the corset') in the U.K., when mortgages were provided, in the main, only by building societies. The philosophy was that banks lent for short-term needs, very often to support business and industry in their production cycles. Building Societies were in the long-term lending business, mainly lending to house-

---

[1] https://www.centralbank.ie/consumer-hub/explainers/what-are-the-mortgage-measures

buyers, though in the 1930s they also supported, usually small, property developers in funding the purchase of land and construction of houses. Yes, building societies were once much more intimately involved in the house*building* sector.

One downside of the previous division of lending between building societies and banks was having to wait for a mortgage offer. Sometimes it meant saving with a building society for a period of time before they would consider you for a mortgage. It sometimes meant that buyers were told that mortgages were not available immediately and they would have to wait a month or so. No politician would dare suggest we return to such forms of rationing of credit.

Banks are invulnerable and will always get away with incontinent lending?

After the 2008 GFC, the financial sector's malfeasance was blatant. Banks were forced to beg the government to bail them out. As many suggest, by doing so, an opportunity to address long-standing problems of the financial sector through radical reformation was missed. The result would have been to ensure banks were brought under tighter control. There may be an impression that banks, having been bailed out, were allowed to continue business as usual by advancing mortgages as before. This was certainly the theme contained in *The Big Short*, the 2015 film starring Christian Bale based on the way in which a small group of maverick investors were able to bet against the US mortgage market based on inherent flaws and corruption they'd identified in research. Notably, the housing market in the

US dropped sharply in 2007 (in anticipation of the crash?). Subsequently, the market continued to trickle down and had declined 20% by 2012. Thereafter, it seemed like it was back to business as usual. Massive mortgage lending and the 'emergency' low rates of interest have driven real house prices back up again to the extent they've now (early 2022) reached pre-crash levels.

There was, however, one small new tax imposed on the banks which held some promise. The "Permanent Bank Levy" was introduced in George Osborne's June 2010 Emergency Budget having been negotiated as part of the Coalition Agreement. Osborne had been in the habit of tacking 'Permanent' to measure in order to distinguish them from Labour's 2009 one-off levy on bankers' bonuses. In his budget speech, Osborne declared the aim of the Bank Levy "is to incentivise a reduction in the use of wholesale finance by banks, with a view to reducing the risk of another financial crisis being triggered by liquidity issues". The Bank Levy was to be "based on total liabilities and equity as shown in the relevant balance sheet," of the 30 or 40 biggest banks. The initial rate was set at 0.07% and was expected to raise "in excess of £2 billion."

It should come as little surprise to learn that the major banks used their influence to whittle away even this tiny percentage. However, it contained the seeds of a brilliant idea, namely *Seigniorage*[1]. This is the benefit that the issuer of currency gains from its production. Banks have the privilege of creating money from 'fresh air'. Osborne's Levy was a first attempt to make them pay for the raw material that's the basis of their business. The hope was that over-production of money, for example, to provide lending for mortgages, would carry a cost to the bank and, as a result would incentivise the banks to be more prudent.

What can we conclude about controlling the banks as a means of slowing down or even stopping house price? Banks and building societies used to obey directives from the Bank of England and were willing to accept controls like the 'Corset'. Not any more. So powerful and influential have the banks become, that it may be impossible to rein them in again. But the basic facts remain:

- Bank lending leads to house price rising far beyond their intrinsic product value
- Lending for house purchase is good business for banks because of the asset value involved.

But what is the 'asset value' that makes any given house worth far more than the value of the product (the house) itself?

---

[1] If Seigniorage and the Bank Levy is new to you one of us has published a paper on the blog of Positive Money about it: https://positivemoney.org/2015/09/george-osbornes-permanent-bank-levy-is-it-seigniorage/

Summary

It was once the case that restraint on banks as mortgage lenders and building societies as the sole source of mortgage finance worked to keep demand in the housing market subdued and house prices stable. A return to this level of control is politically infeasible. Instead we need to look for newer techniques of credit control more in line with the now-widespread understanding of money creation and MMT. Taking back control of our own money and the means of its creation is not going to be easy. We are up against possibly the most powerful lobby of all and they, the Banks, will do all they can to prevent it.

Chapter 7

'Plot Value' is the asset that explains why 'house'-prices vary from place to place

Identical houses located in different parts of the country, even different parts of the same region, sell for different prices. No-one denies that. Houses may be exactly the same, with similar-sized gardens, in similar suburbs, yet their selling price will be different. This is not a matter of small differences. Selling prices in prosperous locations such as Oxford will be *many times* higher than a northern town like Newcastle. We'll present figures on these differences later in the chapter.

Is this because housebuilders are much more efficient in some places? Or could it be that building workers are paid so much less in some parts of the country? Or maybe the raw materials, the sand and gravel, cement, bricks, timber and all other components can be bought more cheaply, with lower transport costs? Analysis shows these factors account for a relatively small amount of the difference in house prices. So, what's the real reason for the difference? As the Channel Four show puts it, "Location! Location! Location!" But what makes the actual plot that a house stands on in one location more valuable than another plot elsewhere? Because the cost of building a house is not what varies, so it must be that for houses old and new it is *the price of the plot of land* on which any house is built that accounts for variation.

Estimating the price of the plot element in the overall sale price of a house

'Comparables' is a technical word used by valuers and estate agents to explain how they estimate the value of, or more usually, a suggested selling price of a house. It's something we can all do these days with the help of websites such as Zoopla or Rightmove. By taking data for selling prices from the Land Registry, these websites provide a basis for estimating a likely selling price by comparison with the prices achieved by similar, comparable properties nearby. If you are a homeowner, we'd be surprised if you haven't already tried this method for yourself in guessing how much your own house is worth. For this exercise we're taking our old favourite, the 1930s Semi. Millions of these were built in all parts of Britain in the housebuilding boom that occurred between the two world wars. Instead of looking nearby for comparables, let's go nation-wide.

Where in the country are the cheapest houses? According to Zoopla it's Shildon in country. Durham[1]. A 1930s 3-bed freehold semi-detached in College Street, Shildon DL4 was on sale in May 2021 at **£120,000.** Like all the other examples about to be quoted it had a virtually identical layout, size and garden, on a pleasant suburban road. That's comparable, then.

---

[1] Revealed: the most affordable areas in Britain - Zoopla Nicky Burridge March 18, 2021Zoopla

So that gives the baseline and here are the prices for comparable semi-detached houses which were for sale in May 2021 in areas of increasing affluence:

3-bed semis	Located in	Sale Price	Plot Premium
Baseline	Shildon, College Street,	£120,000	£0
Moderate Premium	West Park Ave, Northfield, Birmingham	£210,000	£90,000
Medium Premium	Quinton Road Birmingham B17	£375,000	£245,000
High Premium	Marsh Lane Headington Oxford	£475,000	£345,000
Maximum Premium	Sandpits Road, Richmond TW10	£1,095,000	£975,000

This method of inter-regional comparables is straightforward, although it would need to be worked up in much more detail if it had any significant consequences. It is also something well understood by the vast majority of homeowners. So, alternatively we might logically observe, plots are cheap, very cheap, in Shildon but in Richmond, London, a plot even for a modest house costs nearly £1,000,000. We'd acknowledge that this is a quick and dirty exercise to demonstrate that plots are key to understanding house prices. Everyone accepts that the 'location' of any house makes a difference to its price, a difference which can be encapsulated in the value of the plot.

The vast majority of plots are equally served by utilities and access to national and local services. That's not what makes the difference in plot-value. Public transport, roads and schools are of varying quality in relation to any plot but may have some effect. A well-researched example is that of schools; being in the catchment area of a good school adds significantly to the plot value. Access to transport links can make a big difference to plot-value as can the nature of local facilities such as shops and entertainment. But the main difference is relative prosperity of the region. The wealth of a particular area is based on many influences but one, job opportunities and wages that prevail is what creates effective demand. What we may infer is that there's a strong correlation between high wages and high plot values.

So, we contend, the value of a plot of land used for housing derives overwhelmingly from benefits bestowed by society. What we may infer is that there's a strong correlation between high wages and high plot values. Much of this plot-value enhancement is due to public expenditure. High wages are the result of effort and ingenuity by society, collectively. It is this public and collective effort which leads to the claim that "It's Society that gives the plot its Value". Even the added bonus of a pleasant view (or the detraction of a sewage works next door) are part of society's value creation. We created it, but are we all entitled to ask the owners for an annual payback for the benefits bestowed on the plot? The counterargument is that homeowners paid for their house, including the plot, and with a bit of help from the mortgage, so they deserve to keep all of the uplift in value.

Of course planning laws are a factor too. Sometimes the aim is to limit the exploitation of a tract of land, by limiting the number of houses per acre that can be built. On an individual plot there will be limits to the height of a house, and on building out in front, beyond the building line. Economists would argue that this deliberate limitation on maximum exploitation of the plot forces up prices, especially of existing house. But some would go further and say

> "The main cause of this [excess of house prices over build cost] is regulations that ban buildings that make better use of the land."[1]

Their solution, to allow anyone to build anything, anywhere, to abolish all planning laws, is pure fantasy. But they do have a point. *Some* of the excess of plot-value over basic building cost can be explained these restrictions. Nevertheless, *all* of the excess is discoverable from the plot-value.

---

[1] This quote is from a very interesting article on a blog site www.worksinprogress.co/issue/the-housing-theory-of-everything from 14Sep2021

Summary

So the asset that bankers lend on is mainly the value of the plot under the house, a value which derives for society's efforts, not the hard work of the plot holder. Plot-value is the main target of bank-lending. Plots are in limited supply whether by planning rules or slow build-out. Don't blame the banks! They see an easy and very safe lending opportunity, and they pile in. Though they may have been far too enthusiastic in the years immediately prior to the 2008 GFC, freed again by bailouts using public money, they are piling in again. But all credit to the banks. By profligate over-lending they have discovered just how much 'rent' — the economists' term for income earned, not through labour or exchange, rather by extracting the advantages of a monopoly – can be extracted.

Chapter 8

The market for assets; not the standard economic theory

So we've shown that the price of the plot, separate from the house varies from place to place. The cost of producing the building—the house is near-identical in all parts of Britain (apart from some very exotic locations). As houses age they will suffer depreciation and be worth less. Owners may, at a cost, hold off the ravages of time with maintenance, plus replacement with more up-to-date and efficient fittings. Modernisation, such as fitting thermal insulation and solar panels, and extensions can hold off some of the ravages of depreciation.

It would take a very degraded and ineffective industry to produce products that are *worse* than their earlier output, but this almost describes today's housebuilding industry. So the hypothesis that 'older houses, especially well-maintained and up-dated houses are just as good value as brand-new houses' has some merit. Depreciation may be held at bay, but the difference in quoted prices for identical houses in different parts of the town, area or region remains. Only the plot-price explains why prices are so massively different depending on their location.

Land is an asset

As the previous chapter explains, the market price of any house also includes the price of the plot of land on which it stands. Plot value varies hugely, but also encapsulates all the advantages of being in that location. To a large extent it is the affluence of the borough and the region that create the demand and sets the price of the plot, and has little to do with the plot itself. This affluence is a result of the efforts of the people working in this area. Well-paid people can afford the re-payments on bigger mortgages. With their well-earned wealth they can also afford second- or retirement-homes in picturesque locations, which creates its own secondary demand, together with higher plot prices.

That explains the differences in house-prices in different locations. But does it explain the seemingly inexorable *rise* in house prices. This is a rise, remember, in excess of inflation generally, which is subject to sharp spikes, followed by fairly slow falls. But the fall-back is always to a higher level than before and has resulted (in 2022) in average house-prices *eight* times average earnings.

Why should homebuyers have to pay more of their salary for the same house? Why would banks and others wish to lend so much to assist the buyers of a 'house'? The house is just a man-made product, so it can only be the value of the land that makes this worthwhile. Land in the form of a plot to build on costs nothing to produce, yet is sold at large and increasing prices. That's the perfect description of *asset* rather than a *commodity*. Land is of course a sort of monopoly; 'they ain't making land anymore' as the old saying goes. The most important conclusion is that the most significant factor in the price of a house is the price of the plot. That's not a commodity it's an asset. So the standard economic analysis for commodities *do not apply.*

The Economics of Assets in the market

Say 'asset' and perhaps gold or diamonds may be the first thing that come to mind. They have value based on their rarity. Land for housing fits that description too. That also applies to land that's already built on, in spades[1]!. Since only a small additional quantity of land becomes available each year, the result is scarcity and high plot prices. It helps if your asset has low holding costs. Gold may need costly safe storage, but it costs nothing to hold a piece of housing land for as long as you like[2].

The *Land* Registry (note the title) is the official record of your ownership of a piece of land. This record will show the buildings which exists at a time of exchange of ownership. This confers a great deal of security and makes it much more difficult for a fraudster to steal your land and house. You pay fees but have the Government and its legal services to ensure your asset is safe.

Mortgage lenders fully appreciate the characteristics of land under houses. That's why it is such an attractive

---

[1] A phrase popular with Bridge players, although we like the earth-shifting connotations.

[2]Unless the cost of lost interest is included, which could be realised by selling the land and investing the funds raised.

form of collateral for loan. An added benefit is that land can neither be moved away to another location, nor can it be hidden. This is where the self-validating cycle takes hold, and the prices of plots are pushed ever upwards. A shortage of houses for sale enables the better-off to out-bid poorer rivals. Banks are happy to lend because they always have the funds, and they know their borrowers can pay back their loans. The rising market encourages owners to hold off selling, in the hope the market will rise further, thereby reducing supply. All this seems to validate the wisdom of the lender and the canniness of the buyers. Only a sharp reduction in confidence can shake this cycle. But it only works because land is an asset, not a commodity. The new supply to the market is hampered by this essential feature. That is why there is no point in exhorting the housebuilders to 'build more'. The asset that is land is governed by different laws of economics. Normal supply and demand doesn't work.

This is the reason for the jagged 'see-saw' of house-and-land prices after 1970. Banks were given more freedom to lend and used it to continue lending on the minor asset of the house but, in fact, underpinned by the major asset of the plots of land they stood on. The freedom given to the banks and the financial services generally has almost always been one way, more freedom to lend more. This, in turn, explains why 'house'-prices have been on a continual upward trend. The graph in Chapter 1 shows a trend value nominally around 2.5% above inflation. It's the plot-asset that has made investment in British houses a very attractive long term investment.

A house (and land) as an investment: An owner's perspective

More than a century ago only 10% of households owned their home. All others rented from a landlord. The distribution of wealth in the UK was hugely unequal. The gradual rise of home ownership over the century from one in ten to a peak of 70% was accompanied by a downward spread of wealth. Housing as an asset meant that quite ordinary people could own their home and become a part of the 'Great Home-Owning Democracy'. This has produced a tangible, not to say spendable, impact.

How could this new wealth be used? It is almost a cliché that homeowners will say that "it will be nice to leave something to the children". In other words, "It's not much use to me, but it gives me a warm feeling." Such cynicism is only worthy of economists. Putting human values before monetary rewards should be saluted, not derided. Of course, these days, the free equity of older folk in their housing gives an opportunity for an earlier transmission of wealth. This is known colloquially as the 'Bank of Mum & Dad'!

'Equity withdrawal' has become a familiar piece of jargon in recent years. It's difficult to open some newspapers or watch certain television channels without seeing advertisements urging homeowners to extract money from the value of their home. Is this one of the benefits of homeowning? It is sometimes touted as such and undoubtedly *might* be a boon to obtain of a significant 'pot' of cash. But beware! Equity withdrawal deals are simply loans, a mortgage based on the collateral to be found, mostly in the value of the plot. Loans have to be re-paid *with interest.*

Equity withdrawal using a form of mortgage (MEW) is, nevertheless, quite commonly used to increase one's spending power. In times when wages are squeezed, borrowing this way can make up for lost spending power. So great was the amount borrowed as MEW, that consumer spending was boosted by as much as 8% in the early 2000s and the Bank of England nervously kept track of it. Clearly MEW as a means of keeping up a lifestyle unaffordable on wages cannot be a sustainable basis for the economy, long term.

Inertia may lead homeowners to stay in a property long past the time when they might have considered a property more suited to their needs. Older people tend to be sentimental about gardens. Many linger on in large family homes even though maintenance is all but impossible for them. Some stay because they fear losing out on the price-rises which are likely to boost the wealth available to those who inherit what they own. Unfortunately, this may make them vulnerable to losing their housing wealth almost completely. Care home fees which strike some as a 'loser's lottery' are a very major concern for elderly homeowners. In order to assuage the fears of older property owners, Boris Johnson in October 2021 broke a manifesto commitment not to raise taxes.

A big problem with housing wealth as an asset, is that it is not 'fungible'. Unlike assets like shares or even gold, you can't normally sell off a bit of your house. Maybe you can divide up the house into flats and live in one and sell the others. The size and layout of your plot might enable you to sell part of the garden to form a new building plot. It is schemes like this that some like the YIMBY campaign (see their website) propose should be granted planning permission more freely. This could be described as city-cramming, and we have to ask is this what people want? It's difficult to see how it could become popular. Such money-making wheezes may make your own home far less liveable, even if they were possible.

The only real way to make money from the wealth of the plot under your house is to trade down. You can move to a smaller plot/house or move to a part of the country where building land, hence houses, are cheaper. Surprisingly few homeowners take this route, certainly well below 10% each year. The enticing financial returns to owning property have not escaped the notice of buy-to-let landlords. This, as we've seen, also applies to homeowners who need to move elsewhere. If they can afford to, by retaining their original property, turning it over to rental, they can make an investment which many consider as good as paying into a pension fund.

Government legislation and tax regimes encourages a good deal of this such investment though, due to tax changes, has become less attractive in recent years. So, the asset of housing, more particularly the asset-value of the plots under houses, has become a major element of investment funded by the financial services industry. Seeing plot-value as an asset gives a much better explanation for what has happened to house-prices. Best of all, it clears the way for realistic proposals *to stop house prices rising.*

A footnote: Can economic science help you win in asset markets?

Judging by their track record, mainstream economists are no better at predicting the prices of assets than they were at spotting the Great Financial Crash on the horizon in 2007. Everyone wants to win on Wall Street, so economic gurus have been happy to oblige. Theories to explain markets for assets include The Efficient Markets Hypothesis (EMH) and Capital asset pricing model (CAPM). A most public and glaring failure was a Wall Street firm called Long-Term Capital Management L.P. (LTCM). They were a hedge fund and employed two economics Nobel prize winners, Myron Scholes and Robert C. Merton. Their Nobels had been awarded for their theories of asset pricing. Their formulas led to initial success, with huge annual returns up to 1998. However, in 1998 they lost $4.6 billion in less than four months. The fund was liquidated and dissolved in early 2000. (based on Wiki). So much for the cleverest of economic scientists!

Instead, the economist Steve Keen suggests that Behavioural Finance, Fractal Markets Hypothesis, IN-efficient Market Hypothesis, Econo-physics may show some promise. None have really worked. Perhaps it is the presence of actual human beings in the management-of-funds process that means behaviour can never be predicted. Doubtless snake-oil salesmen will claim AI will fix it!

So we are stuck with land as an asset, prices which depend on the liberalisation of the finance sector, and greedy owners, including the fabled NINJAs hoping for a free lunch. Our theory is that land as an asset has to be decontaminated, de-commissioned taken out of the market. The remaining questions are: How to do it? And Who is to benefit from this enormous if largely hypothetical mountain of wealth?

Chapter 9

The next step: Unbundling the price of the building from the cost of the plot

The characteristic of an asset is that its price can rise and fall irrespective of intrinsic value. In the case of plot-values or house-building land generally this is one asset price that seems only ever to rise, despite some ups and downs[1].

Previously, in Chapter 6, it was suggested that reducing the lenders' freedom to create unlimited mortgages was one way of bringing some stability in house prices and preventing further rises. One obvious snag is that this would have an equally calming effect on the commodity part of the loan as well as the plot value. Lending to support more spending on the actual house is a good thing and cannot get out of hand because of the competition to create value in such commodities. Lending for purchase of the asset which is the plot of land has had a dire effect. Asset prices can be inflated almost without limit. Speculative bubbles, large rises and falls in prices are characteristic of asset markets.

---

[1] There is an excellent chart which shows this at blogs.lse.ac.uk/politicsandpolicy/land-prices-the-dog-thats-lost-its-bark

Separating land values from house values

Could some means be contrived to separate out the marketing for the sales, production and design of the house itself away from the way the title for plot of land under it is conveyed (that's legal jargon for passing on ownership)? Our next big step is to examine ways in which plots under existing houses and land for house-building can be taken out of the speculative asset market. This may sound both an unfamiliar and frankly dangerous intervention, but please bear with us. In fact, such ideas have been around for centuries and have always been part of economic theory.

Chapter 10

Common ownership of land—Community Land Trusts: A proposal with potential

Community and trust suggest some moral superiority, far away from profit-maximising financiers. If only there were some public-spirited person or group of locals who bought up a parcel of land and used is to build houses for the locals. Keep the land-profit local and stop the banks bidding up the price of our local asset. Such noble sentiments have, in a small number of cases been taken a bit further. In a very earnest paper from the New Economics Foundation (NEF) in 2017 it was noted:

> *Community Land Trusts (CLTs) are non-profit, community-based organisations that develop housing or other assets at permanently affordable levels for long-term community benefit. A CLT typically does this by* ***separating the value of the building from the land that it stands on.*** *[our emphasis added]*

This is exactly what was indicated in the last chapter. The paper continues, suggesting that this is something of a charitable enterprise:

> *The land is owned by the CLT and people purchase or rent the homes that sit on it. Because*

they only need to purchase or rent the building and not the land, a CLT home is more affordable than a conventional home

'Affordable' is a buzz word frequently bandied about in housing discussions. What it really means is that it is rented or sold at 'less than the full market price'. Economists would call this subsidised housing, with tenants or owners obtaining the benefit of a home cheaper than others are likely prepared to pay. The CLT could deliberately lay off charging full market rent for the house and land. So, it should be stressed, this is subsidised, not affordable housing. The authors go on to suggest that the operation could still be profitable. Of course it would! There is a huge amount of unearned rent to be found under neally all the houses in the UK! So long as revenue is in excess of operating cost, the report continues, the excess should be used to improve the neighbourhood. If such trusts were run as democratic owner-or tenant-co-operatives, then they could decide where the money should be spent.

A more generalised version of a CLT which acted in a more conventional business-like manner, is the main suggestion in this NEF paper. They would charge for the land values in full:

> *The CLT would levy a Land Usage Charge (LUC) upon all occupiers of land proportionate to the land's locational (and use) value. The profits generated by the LUC would then be distributed for the benefit of all members of the CLT, through investment in*

infrastructure, or through dividends to individuals, or a combination of these.

There's a lot more explanation, but the core message is clear. Take away land values from the market, especially as collateral for mortgages. By doing this, the wealth encapsulated in on land can be retained within the community and used accordingly. It's accepted that CLTs would effectively be isolated islands in estates 'swimming' in a vast ocean of individual owner-occupiers. The owners who buy their house would retain the unrealised value of the inflated price of their plots of land. So it might be many years before CLTs affect the market, and influence land prices.

Nonetheless, there's hope. If CLTs thrive, potential homeowners would see the financial benefits of this model. Eventually, as land is de-collateralised and bank lending limited by reduction in land-lending opportunities, the broken housing market could be reformed. Better, cheaper housing, and lots of it could result. In this endeavour we wish the proponents of CLTs every success.

An early version of this ideal exists already in places such as Letchworth Garden City and Bournville Estate, Birmingham. The land was acquired for benevolent purposes and a strict regime of beautiful layouts and views was dictated. The irony is that today these houses are privately owned, and sell at a premium because properties were well built, including aesthetic additions, and local environment perceived to be extremely attractive. For more information on this attractive idea see Josh Ryan-Collins

2017 et al *Modern Land Reform* in a paper published by the New Economics Foundation.

Chapter 11

Nationalising all housing land for the public benefit

Kevin McCloud in *The Guardian* on 13th September 2021 finds it "iniquitous and hugely corrosive" that land values in the UK are so high because companies are hoarding land and only drip-feeding it into the market. "What's really needed is a complete radical state-controlled distribution of land and a removal of land profit from the equation. That sounds nuts and Stalinistic, but it's exactly what happens in Germany," McCloud explains. Moreover, he continues, "Since the war, our planning system unwittingly has worked in cahoots with capitalism to create an unsustainable development economy." As McCloud asserts, the UK is "pretty much" the only country in the world to have so few major construction companies dominating the market for housing. He also notes that they build the most cramped houses in Europe:

> *If you're a housebuilder, the only way you can make some money and sell a house people can afford is to build really small ones. It's awful.*

Kevin McCloud is correct to suggest the ownership of all the land by the state would be Stalinistic (it's Communism, actually!) So, even though advocating taking all housing land, including the land under existing houses, into public ownership sounds extremely harsh, at least it would completely solve the mortgage collateral problem. With no land or plot value to lend on, only the value of the building could stand as collateral. As we said in the last chapter, mortgaging would become another branch of consumer lending just like the market for motor cars.

In the old days it was aristocrats and other wealthy inheritors who owned most of the land. Most UK industrial towns and cities were developed under the aegis of a great landowner who leased land for the houses for a fixed period, usually 99 years. Some of the landowners took pains to ensure that their 'estates' were well laid out and maintained their value. Examples include Calthorpe and Cadbury in Birmingham and the Westminster, London estate owned by a Duke, in London.

In time, leasehold became a purely financial arrangement. 'Ground rents' fixed at the commencement of sales of houses, were eroded in value due to inflation over the years. Eventually, these bore little resemblance to the underlying value of the plot. Legislation on leasehold enfranchisement led to the breakup of estates.

Echoes of this system can be found in the practices of today's housebuilders. New homes are, in some cases, being sold with leases which have 'escalator' clauses. Starting with modest ground rents of a few hundred pounds, the lease specifies something like the doubling of the payment every 10 years. This has led to outraged homebuyers discovering that their new homes are virtually unsaleable. As a consequence, moves to outlaw such practice and compensate losers are being rushed through Parliament.

Could a municipality or local authority own and develop housebuilding land? This is what actually happened in the case of estates of council houses for rent. As a policy rents did not reflect the current land value and remained low through 'historic cost pooling'. This could be described as benign landowners failing to extract the maximum ground-rent, in this case as a form of social support. One prime example shows how local-authority ownership of land and leasehold development can be of great financial benefit. In the case of Milton Keynes, a vast tract of land was compulsorily purchased at farmland prices (this practice was later outlawed, and the full development price had to be paid elsewhere). The uplift in land value then accrued to the new town development of Milton Keynes, and also involved a great deal of private housing.

Internationally, two outstanding examples stand out as shining beacons in the housing market, Hong Kong and Singapore. *The Economist* magazine is lavish in its praise of Singapore. It alone seems to have solved the housing market conundrum of providing good quality housing at reasonable prices, and in abundance. Hong Kong does pretty well on housing, too. But one peculiarity is that in both these places, the *state owns all the land. There are no freeholders.* Andrew Purves[1], who's from an old Hong Kong banking family, has researched this unusual arrangement, and continues to investigate that paragon of housing virtue that is Singapore.

---

[1] In his 2015 book *No Debt, High Growth, Low Tax: Hong Kong's Economic Miracle Explained*

That all land in Hong Kong is owned by the state is a colonial relic. Singapore was slightly different. After Singaporean independence, the government already owned much of the developmental land. The government then took steps to take over ownership of the vast majority (90%+) of all the land on the island. So, in both regimes, housing developed as a state-organised leasehold system. There are many advocates of Community Land Trusts who would like to replicate the Singaporean model but, crucially, on a mutual basis. Many policy wonks [1] find this an attractive idea, (see Brett Christophers, 2018). Therefore, we believe, a call to nationalise all house-building land, including the land under existing houses, may not be such a crazy idea as some would claim.

[1] Those who taking enthusiastic or excessive interest in the specialised details of a particular subject or field, especially political policy

Chapter 12

Transform all other property taxes to a single plot value charge.

Following on from the explanation in previous chapters, it's easy to see how the plot value varies in different parts of the country. As we acknowledge, these variation in plot-values depend, in the main, on the economic vigour of the locality, transport links, and the attractiveness of the neighbourhood. Imagine then, a charge being levied on the value of each plot as if it were a capital sum being invested in a perfectly safe (gilt-edged is the jargon) bank or building society? In normal times you might expect a return of two or three per cent, plus inflation. Granted, these are not normal times, and interest rates have been at near-zero for over a decade, but this surely will not last. Another approach might be to link the rate charged to the average interest rate (APRC) on mortgages. At the moment (Jan2022) that's a more realistic 3-3½%.

This hypothetical 3% of plot-value charge would have the effect of reducing the 'house-price' to the price/value of the house building alone. The market value of any house, made from the bricks-and-mortar, fixtures fittings, structure and the rest, would represent its building cost less depreciation. Houses that were more or less identical (or very similar), would have the same price tag regardless of which part of the country they're located.

This is what's generally meant by full **land**-value taxation. Since we're only dealing with the plots under and around houses, let's call this a plot-value charge (PVC) to distinguish it from land tax in general. This is our preferred option for 'levelling down' the price of identical houses to the cheapest in the land and thereby making homes affordable for all. It sounds like a terrible deal for existing home owners, but remember this is only a thought experiment. No politician would be mad enough to propose anything like this, although Jeremy Corbyn once was[1], falsely of course!

The fortunate owner of the semi in Richmond, London has house on a plot that is 'worth' £975,000. This is based on the assumption that the price of a plot in Shildon plot is trivial compared to the house price. If PVC is set at 3%, the owner in Shildon, Co Durham would pay nothing. However, the Richmond homeowner would have to pay £29,250 per annum for a 3% PVC. This is levelling down with a vengeance.

There is a current campaign advocating something along these lines called Fairer Share (/fairershare.org.uk/proportional-property-tax/) They propose that council tax be levied at the same percentage rate on all dwellings throughout the land as a means of 'levelling up' (a favourite Tory government slogan). Good luck to them, but it's difficult to see this becoming party policy anytime soon.

---

[1] DailyMail 'Labour Plan to Crash House Prices' 7June2017

PVC may be a purely hypothetical idea, but has a long provenance. As long ago as 1909, the Liberal Chancellor Lloyd George, energetically assisted by Home Secretary Winston Churchill, passed into law such a tax. More recently, in Ireland, following the Financial Crash, they came very close to introducing something similar in 2013[1]. LVT/PVC has its advocates still.

There would be some compensations for the homeowner in such a proposal. All other forms of tax on property such as stamp duty on sales, council tax, most of Inheritance Taxes could be abolished. Best of all, the hated practice of seizing value in property to pay for exorbitant care-home fees could cease. Advocates of land value tax claim that such would be the amount of revenue generated, that even income tax and national insurance could be lowered as well.

Another way in which the cost of a full PVC could be lessened is a bit is more subtle. Remember the purpose of a full 'Plot Value Charge' is to separate and extinguish plot value from house-prices. Perhaps we can *thank* the banks and their incontinent lending on house purchase for discovering what is the absolute maximum price (rent in the jargon) they can extract through mortgage lending. In a dynamic situation where the PVC rises to achieve parity of house (the building) prices nationwide, the actual values of the plots and hence the amount to pay will almost certainly be considerably less. This is shown by the experience of local

---

[1] Jim O'Leary September 2018 *How (Not) To Do Public Policy: Water Charges and Local Property Tax* . Galway, NUI; Whitaker Institute for Innovation & Societal Change.

authorities and the Chinese islands of Hong Kong and Singapore, according to Andrew Purves.

That's the theory. What's actually being proposed?

The theme of this book is explicitly about *stopping* further price rises, not levelling down all house-prices to the lowest in the country. Falling house prices would, in the short-term, be devastating for many. So many mortgages are already in place, with values close to 100% of the price paid, that a downturn in prices would return many, possibly millions, to the misery of negative equity experienced in the early 1990s.

Is there is a modest level of PVC which removes a small proportion of the land value out of harm's way, and yet puts the brakes on further house price rises? Perhaps a PVC of one-tenth of the full 3% would suffice, though further research is needed. What is certain is that any rate of PVC will have a braking effect on the plot-value element of house prices.

Residents of Richmond in London may relax. They won't be asked for £29,250 a year to pay this new house-price stabilisation levy. Something like £3,000 per year or probably less, will be all we ask, and with it comes the added benefit that maybe other nasty taxes would be abolished to compensate. A possible scenario for this will be proposed in the chapter after the next.

Chapter 13

Housing possibilities for our grandchildren[1]: Something to look forward to.

A Scenario for the near future, when the once-broken housing market is now thriving, prices have stopped rising and dropped back to their true worth.

The main theme of this book is that of stabilising house prices and ensuring they do not rise any more, an objective we consider both necessary and urgent. But we can dream! Once stable prices have been achieved using the mechanisms described in the previous chapters, it becomes clear we can go further. The whole business of plot values can be completely separated out and dealt with outside the market. Eventually buying a house will become exactly that, buying the building, as a commodity like, for instance, a car.

Back in the 1960s it was quite normal for couples in their 20s to buy a new house. The houses may have been very flimsy, shoddy affair, and on soul-less estates. By the

---

[1] This is of course a shameless crib of the famous *Economic Possibilities for our Grandchildren* from 1930 by John Maynard Keynes He peered 100 years into the future and got many things wrong. We're only looking 20 or 30 years ahead and hope to do better!

next generation few could afford a home of their own until they were in their 30s or 40s, which takes us up to the 2000s. Any affordable new house was tiny, although it was a bit more thermally efficient. For those settling down to raise a family the costs were painful, so expensive, that it might cost five times their annual earnings even though they were both nearly 40! The only way they could raise the deposit was by getting your grandparents to dig into their savings—the bank of Mum and Dad just to pay for the deposit.

Perhaps we should explain a bit more about the crooked bargain the politicians made with the home-owning public, how that has now all changed for the better, starting with a small change in taxation and banking back in 2024.

Back then, as has always been the case, the obvious reason for buying a home was to find somewhere to live. It may have been a bit pokey and shoddy and very expensive. Typically, first-time buyers have to pay out as much as 30 or 40 percent of their after-tax wages to pay for the mortgage. But you did have the status of 'homeowner'. You were now a member of the Great Home Owning Democracy. Mortgaged or not, this applied even if you are a lease holder, but it is even better to be a freeholder.

Now that all seems a bit abstract. Home owning democracy indeed. Actually, there was a much stronger reason to 'get your foot on the bottom rung of the property ladder' as they used to call it. By owning a home, you could look forward to becoming rich (on paper anyway). **Capital gains,** was the lure. That was wealth gained without working for it, wealth created by house price inflation. As a young first-time buyer, you might have been spending a huge proportion of income — up to half — to 'get on the (free money) ladder'. But as time passed the repayments reduced and the equity—the value of your house *minus* the mortgage outstanding—increases. Result!

The first quite small change came back in 2024, when Stamp Duty, as it was quaintly called, was switched to a form of land-value tax that we now call Plot Value Charge. It took time for the new reality of partial PVC to sink in. Perhaps one reminder ('nudge' in today's socio-speak), came from the money lenders. They were well aware of the reduced 'equity' caused by this partial tax of the value of the land under the house and started offering less by way of mortgage.

The next change followed the care home fees scandal. In September 2021 the then Chancellor Rishi Sunak who eventually became Britain's first non-white Prime Minister, had announced an entirely merited funding boost for the NHS and the Social Care system. In part this was to soften the blow felt by many families when frail elderly people had to go into a care home. To pay the huge fees, many were forced to sell their family home. The funding boost was intended to stop this, or at least reduce its impact.

To pay for this the Chancellor had chosen to tax younger workers by raising their rates of National Insurance, a form of income tax in reality. This was what caused the scandal! Once the effects of the new higher taxes on the incomes of workers kicked in there were mass protests. So, the government bit the bullet, cancelled the tax rises, and offered a small plot-value charge to the elderly who wished to dodge the fees. After all, if protecting older homeowners' property from seizure to pay care home fees was the aim, then surely a small levy on property values was the fairest way to do it? It was hugely popular and soon more than 85% over the over-60s were enrolled in this new plot-value charge.

Subsequently, in a populist gesture the much-feared inheritance tax became voluntary on the bit related to house-values. All homeowners had to do was enrol for another small addition to their PVC. This was to satisfy a virulent campaign run by the rich under the banner of the Taxpayers' Alliance. Thus, by the late 2020s most houses were paying some kind of PVC. The final *coupe de grace* was expected when the few remaining holdouts were compulsorily subject to PVC. This first stage brought home to the owners a new awareness of the nature of house prices. Specifically, that house prices don't actually rise, only the value of the land on which they're built. At long last politicians 'got it', that using the tax system to hold down the price of houses was popular and a vote-winner.

Gradually a new piece of conventional wisdom would be draped over the consciousness of homeowners: Instead of the inane Kirstie Allsopp refrain, that "House prices always go up", we started to hear, "A house is effectively a manufactured product which loses value from the day it's built. Now that Land Values are being taxed away by PVC, for the benefit of us all, only a fool expects house prices to do anything other than fall."

Once the various forms of plot-value charge were bundled together from the Stamp Duty, plus the eldercare insurance and scrapping of inheritance tax, it resulted in about 50% of the plot value being taken out of the price of houses generally. In the short run, this certainly gave the builders a firm nudge to get on with it and use their land bank to build. The same applied to empty houses in disrepair awaiting development, which added a bit to the output of new-build.

Then a new idea caught on. Nowadays, in the 2020s when homeowners are asked what they intended to do with all the wealth they had accumulated in their property, many would reply "To leave something for the children." As a result many feared downsizing not least because they (or their children) might lose out on future price rises. Once the anticipated price rises had been eliminated a new attitude set in. "Do we really need this large family house, now that the family have moved on?" The nine million or so owner-occupier who have paid off their mortgage used to have little incentive to downsize. This was just the nudge that was required. This is one way in the future that a vast new and effective supply would arrive on the housing market, and more supply still means lower prices

In the wider economy things were changing too. The Chancellor of the Exchequer decide to use her existing powers to beef up the Permanent Bank Levy. Banks and other lenders were then gently forced to apply more caution to their lending portfolio, the bulk of which used to be in mortgages. Instead, and to the surprise of many, investing in the booming building and manufacturing sectors had become much more profitable.

This was just what the Georgists (advocates of land tax) had predicted. Shifting the tax burden from incomes and the profits of production onto the value of land and other natural resources frees up a lot of dynamism. Higher incomes, and more of them, but less income tax led to higher tax revenues, lower social costs such as unemployment and lower pay-outs on housing benefits which had been a huge chunk of wasteful government expenditure in the old days. A benign cycle had been set off.

But just freeing up more of the existing housing stock, and bringing it on to the market was not enough. The politicians and backward thinking economists were not completely wrong when they said "Build more houses" is the way of fixing the broken housing market. What they missed out was the crucial first step of normalising the market by dealing with the asset-based speculation caused by plot values. So building more, many more new houses was always necessary, but raised the ultimate question: Where are we going to build them? and: Is the building industry capable, can they build it cheaply and in large volumes?

When plot value charging was applied to the landbanks held by the housebuilders it nudged them into more building. The increased supply was welcome but didn't slow down the prices rises by much. The volume builders of those days still preferred the large estate developments using their slow build-out marketing technique. But changes were afoot. There was a mini-boom in one-off plots, where one typically-sized house or bungalow (which was just 90 square metres in those days), was knocked down and replaced with two or sometimes three 'town houses', each of which was at least 50% larger than the old average. Some entrepreneurial housebuilders got quite slick at this plot recycling, getting the turnaround time down to 12 weeks in some cases.

One very popular move was known as the corner-plot bungalow switch. Typically a grannie living in a bungalow on a big corner plot, liked where she lived and didn't want to move. So the builders made her an offer – go on a free six-week cruise (by this time cruising was felt safe again after the Covid shock). While she was away the new rapid-build process developed by the Chinese swung into action. When she returned four beautiful, cosy yet spacious new homes had been built on her old plot, all filled with technology she could only marvel at. One of them was a first floor flat, slightly smaller than her old bungalow. Two large four-bed houses had also been comfortably fitted in next door. Best of all they were so thermally efficient were they that fuel bills were close to zero!

Politicians quickly cottoned on to the fact that even a partial plot value charge worked well, produced the goods, made houses cheaper, made room for a huge new housebuilding industry. Most of the electors were clamouring for more PVC, especially to get rid of the hated Council Tax. They liked the possibility of a nice new cheap-to-run larger house. Even the environmentalists cheered when the old, draughty heat-wasting 1930s semis started to be replaced by larger comfy homes and lots of them. When in the end we finished up with full PVC, we had houses which cost the same in all parts of England. Only the amount of PVC differs from place to place.

There's lots of new or fairly new places to live out there. Some have argued that with just four major builders dominating the whole market for new houses, homes have become a bit 'samey'. Nobody ever said that in the old days about cars, did they? If you wanted one of those embarrassing SUVs, they all looked the same, but did that matter? Not a bit! They were well-built reliable cars and all had lots of useful features. The customers were delighted, had excellent value for money, and didn't mind a bit when they noticed another car identical to theirs.

The same goes for housing. These (future, imaginary) days you can buy a pretty nifty well-designed hi-spec home of around 150 square metres these days for about £150,000 in 2022 money. How did the builders become so efficient, and how do they manage to build out so many delightful new homes in so many different specifications? Quite simple really. Freed from the burden of being land speculators they were able to concentrate on their proper job of building better houses more efficiently and lots of them. In this they have succeeded admirably (We won't bore you with the technical details). The result has been that nowadays buyers much prefer new houses because they are so much better.

Of course not everybody is happy. Consider the parents of the grandchildren to whom this chapter is addressed. They were looking forward to becoming richer year by year. In their early married years, when you were born, they had to really stretch their spending to pay for the over-sized mortgage. But they knew, or at least hoped, that it would all be worth it with a big nest egg to live off or pass on when they got to retirement in their 70s. Seeing their dreams of wealth evaporate did make them very grumpy, and some still hanker after the old days.

So, did the middle-class dream of acquiring some wealth die because of something as simple yet so game-changing as plot-value charging? Perhaps a dream of wealth through home-owning for the upper half of society was always a cruel trick to play on the lower half. But the middle classes have sharp elbows and know how to complain. But nowadays these self-same middle classes – the bourgeoisie as Marx called them – still have wealth, but social wealth in the form of excellent health services as well as financial services organised for all like home insurance. And the booming economy has provided wonderful investment opportunities.

The prudent middle classes have as always saved, and unit trusts, shares and even government bonds are held widely throughout society. That is a much healthier form of economic democracy. The politicians have helped, too, by making modest-sized portfolios tax-free, and easy to manage with minimal bureaucracy.

Waiting until you are old to have money, to be rich, to spend on life's luxuries was a moronically stupid idea. Having more of your own money to spend on fun, while you can still enjoy it is a much better idea. Thank goodness for plot-value charging and the wisdom of the politicians in reining in the banks.

Chapter 14

When Grand Theory meets Hard Reality:

Who will Do What It Takes to Stop House Prices Rising?

So much for the future fantasies! Let's leave the task of completely fixing today's broken housing market to one side. The first, and really quite urgent, need is to stop house prices rising. As we've said, there are <u>three</u> practical, eminently doable methods of successfully achieving this:

- Squeeze the banks to restrict their lending on mortgages, or
- Move towards taking housing land, including under existing houses into public ownership, or
- Start taxing away a small part of the plot value under all houses

Which one is best, and how to deal with the politics involved? In the following section we'll deal with what seem to be the main reasons why many believe that stopping house prices is not something they'd welcome.

But some of us *like* rising house prices.

There are voters who like rising house prices. There are powerful interest groups who stand to gain from continued price rises. They will be the opposition who squeal loudly but, more importantly, will happily vote enthusiastically to keep things as they are. The question that may be asked is does anyone *want* house prices to become affordable? Certainly, not the older homeowners who feel wealthier as a result. They believe they've worked hard all their life to pay for their home. They have spent fortunes on repairs, maintenance and, in many cases, modernisation and expensive alterations. 'Don't tell us about the unearned uplift in value of the plot caused by excessive bank lending. We paid for it, it's ours.' is a typical attitude.

This matters intensely because of voting patterns. As a broad generalisation, homeowners and the elderly are much more likely to vote Conservative. Additionally, they are much more likely to vote. On the contrary, renters and younger voters prefer Labour, but are far less enthusiastic when it comes to turning out and actually voting. There is still a majority of owner-occupiers (60%+) so the incentives for politicians are obvious. Conservatives will strongly oppose anything which smacks of house price control. Labour politicians must also appeal to some homeowners so are equally wary of upsetting the 'applecart'.

The financial industry, banks and the like, wield enormous, if mostly unseen, influence. They will be very keen to defend their lucrative mortgage business, even if stopping house-price rises would only take away a small part of it. They can see where price control, if successful, could lead. They may be chastened a bit by their monstrous behaviour in the run-up to the 2008 GFC, linked as it was to sub-prime mortgages, but not sufficiently to radically change their behaviour.

Where is the constituency for limiting house price rises? Chloe Timperley whose excellent book *Generation Rent,* fondly imagines that younger voters forced to pay excessive rent for inadequate accommodation, frequently under extremely unfair conditions, will eventually rise up against this. Perhaps literally. Riots in the streets would certainly be a wake-up call for politicians though it's difficult to see that 'generation rent', as a self-identifying group, would come out and visibly make their displeasure known. Therefore, even if the omens for reining in house price rises are not good, perhaps we can rely on intelligent and knowledgeable politicians, as well as their highly educated advisors, to spot the perils of letting prices run amok, and make some changes that won't ruffle too many voters' feathers.

Squeeze the banks: Fix 1

Advising banks to limit mortgage availability could be tried. It won't work like it did in the 1960s, because banking has changed beyond recognition. A feeble attempt to do so in Ireland didn't work very well (see Ch6). Limiting mortgage availability can be hard on youngsters without a good record of jobs or earnings. Those in the 'gig-economy' would find it particularly difficult to secure a mortgage. Perhaps George Osborne's Permanent Bank Levy offers a way out. How about giving the banks some incentive? Make the Levy adjustable in line with house prices? If house prices go up 10%, the Levy would rise by a similar percentage. Since the Levy is already quite small, 0.07%, an added 10% only takes it up to 0.077%. This seems eminently fair since mortgage lending is the ultimate driving force behind the rise in price of the asset underpinning the house. There would be a bonus too for the bankers. If prices *fell*, then the levy would be that much less. Economists are very keen on these automatic stabilisers.

To do this, to turn bankers into promoters of price stability is technically easy. A simple announcement in the Budget is all it would take. But what if it really worked and house prices really did start to tumble because banks were lending less in the form of mortgages? As we saw in Chapter 5, almost all money in circulation, over (97%), is created by bank lending, most on in terms of 'retail banking' (some 80%), in the form of mortgages.

Would a significant reduction in money lent as mortgages lead to an insufficient supply of money in the economy? No. Any shortfall of money in circulation could easily be made up by some form of QE. Maybe next time it's needed, we'd hope that money is directly handed to us, the citizens in the form of a Universal Basic Income.

Nationalising all the land under houses Fix 2

This looks awful. An Englishman's home is no longer his/her castle. It is indeed a form of communism. However, it can be softened by calling it Community Land or a Land Trust. Ownership by Local Authorities with ground rent paid on municipal leases may be more benign. It will always be tempting for these public-good trusts to limit ground rents to below full market rates.

The 'social' ground landlords may be content with the revenue they receive, and not seek to maximise returns. All this does is create unexploited rent which will result in large positive plot values being left to the leaseholder and not being collected. This is what happened in Hong Kong because the authorities, even the colonial ones did not realise what the system was. (Purves, 2015). So Hong Kong has a house-price boom, too, because full ground rent is left uncollected. There is also the danger of corruption and favouritism when agents within the land-owning public authority can make decisions. Strict and unambiguous rules and close oversight is needed to ensure integrity.

Land Value Tax Methods – in this case a Full Plot-Value Charge Fix3

There is a vast literature around land value taxation, and there are even some small examples of it in use. Despite the fact that economists of all stripes think it's a good tax, better than most, most commentators shy away from it because of the practical problems of implementing it. Here's a few:

- a. Valuation of Land separate from the building is too difficult and won't be understood by taxpayers
- b. Values not being kept up-to-date. For Plot Value charging to work, it must be based on current values. Politicians are always prone to put tricky re-valuations off for the most trivial of reasons. An out-of-date PVC will not properly reflect the purpose of stopping house prices rising
- c. The asset-rich, cash-poor homeowner. A hoary old chestnut. The case of the old person living on in their large old family home is always trotted out as the 'killer objection'. But, of course, there are ways around this. A

government-sponsored honest equity withdrawal could easily be arranged

- d. The politically influential home-owning bourgeoisie. The hard-working middle classes who have scrimped all their lives to pay the mortgage and now find themselves sitting on an extremely valuable asset. Why should they be penalised? Several comments on this. No, they didn't earn it through hard work. Housing wealth is difficult to mobilise, then usually in older years, or through expensive equity withdrawal loans

The political opponents to plot value charging are well aware of what it means, a massive distribution of the tax burden away from workers' salaries onto unearned rental income. Consider what happened when a tiny *hint* of LVT appeared on the agenda. To repeat the warning, according to Carol Wilcox, an academic, and member of a Labour Party group advocating LVT writing in the Morning Star (Aug2018):

> *When the 2017 Labour Party Manifesto contained a small reference to LVT, the Tory Party and its obedient media servants went to town the week before the Election on Labour's "Garden Tax" - which [they claimed] would treble Council Tax and decimate house prices. The irony is that the paper they quoted from, gleaned from the Labour Land Campaign website, clearly stated that the implementation proposed was designed to avoid both those outcomes.*

We may take comfort from the vehemence of this attack. Clearly, trying to reclaim the unearned wealth created by land-value inflation has touched a raw nerve. This suggest that such a tax really will work and reduce the gap in wealth between the very rich and the rest of us. True, there's a large group of homeowners who would feel they were losing out, but most have a relatively small amount at stake. The million-pound home-plot owners are the minority.

Chapter 15

Let's make a small start — change one bad property tax to PVC and watch house prices levelling down

A very effective campaign called Fairer Share emerged in 2020. It called for the replacement of Stamp Duty and local Council Tax by a single national proportional property tax based on the value of each property. Through a series of well-targeted media interventions, this campaign has gained traction with several MPs from all parties expressing support. It's a great idea, not too distant from the plot-value charging proposed here but, sadly, prospects of it getting through our political system and becoming law are virtually nil. It's too ambitious.

Calling for changes in Council Tax reminds politicians of the Poll Tax fiasco. Switching a local tax to a national tax goes against the popular slogan of 'keeping it local'. Worst of all there would be the winners and losers in this switch. Those who would pay less will be quietly comforted, but the small proportion who will be expected to pay more (despite a proposed cap) will be furious. When it comes to tax changes it is the strident voice of the losers that is heard. The winners generally keep quiet. So here's a proposal which is both modest and practical and would be a first step on the way to taking plot-value out of house-prices.

Take one unpopular tax on property and replace it with a *small* amount of Land Value Tax.

When asked[1], the great British public thought that the most unfair tax is that which is imposed on what they may inherit. Next in descending order comes stamp duty, the Television Licence, fuel duty, and Value Added Tax. Taxes on cigarettes and alcohol were deemed 'fair', as was National Insurance and Income Tax. Surprisingly, even council tax was considered fair-ish which should act as warning of the political pitfalls in store for those wanting to switch to LVT.

So, would getting rid 'Death Duties', Inheritance Tax, IHT is the usual abbreviation, be the canniest political move[2]? IHT is certainly the most hated tax, so a switch to LVT might be easy. We will make a suggestion for abolishing IHT later on, but for now, let's stick with Stamp Duty, or Stamp Duty Land Tax (SDLT) to give it its full official name in England. This should be the best and easiest tax to abolish and switch to LVT. As a bonus it even has 'Land Tax' in its name!

---

[1] https://yougov.co.uk/news/2013/02/21/majority-support-mansion-tax/

[2] Note the irony: It was the same 1909 People's Budget that passed both Death Duties and LVT. LVT was later dropped, but Death Duties survived.

The politics of SDLT

In an odd way, Stamp Duty (SDLT) is 'voluntary', you only pay it if you choose to buy a house. SDLT also seems 'fair' because it's directly linked to the price paid to the owner of the house being purchased. The Chancellor of the Exchequer gets away with it because, at any one time, relatively few voters are hit by SDLT. Usually, no more than a million houses change hands each year. Chancellor Osborne (2010-2016) was particularly cavalier with SDLT, changing the rates frequently and, as a result, gaining political kudos by imposing draconian rates on buy-to-lets and million-pound plus mansions. Unlike Thatcher's Poll Tax in the early 1990s, there were no mass protests in the streets against these steep rises in the top rates of SDLT.

The Economics of SDLT

Because it is paid up-front, house-buyers lose out. This discourages sellers too, with fewer houses being put on the market. Employment economists have identified SDLT as a 'drag' on the jobs-market, stifling transactions. In an ideal world, workers would face few impediments to moving to where the jobs are. If this involves selling your house and buying another, SDLT is a further disincentive which discourages free movement of labour. Since SDLT is imposed on buyers every time they purchase a house, it's especially onerous on those who frequently move while changing jobs. So SDLT is both unpopular politically and a tax which badly warps market incentives. It is ripe for reform or replacement, but abolishing altogether would mean losing a very traditional, long-accepted tax.

How best to bring in the new mini-LVT

At the next Budget it would be a straightforward to announce:

As from next May 1st domestic property transfers will no longer be subject to Stamp Duty. Instead, there will be an annual levy on the land-value of the property being sold of one-third of one percent.

The proposed mini-LVT replacement would, like SDLT, be a 'voluntary' tax, and would be a clean break with the old Stamp Duty. There would be no need for parallel trial running. Accordingly, the campaign slogan to sell the change might take the form of:

House-buyers: Don't pay a big lump of SDLT now! Spread your payments out as a yearly charge of just one-third of one percent of the value of the plot of land your house is built on!

Where did the figure of one-third of a percent of the land value come from? We can assume that the Chancellor of the Exchequer aims to be 'revenue neutral' and generate as much in tax revenue, about £8.5 billion, from the new mini-LVT as the old Stamp Duty did previously. We've done the calculations and a third of one percent levy on the value of the land would soon produce the same revenue stream as before.[1] There will be one sting in the tail. Annual revaluation of plot value is the key to making this work as a price-rise stopper. That needs to be explained at the time of

---

[1] Detailed calculations in an article on CB's http://www.conallboyle.com/housing/HsgMnyLandIndex.html of how I worked out the LVT which could be substituted for the one-off SDLT

its introduction. This leads to the sweetener: if house-price rises, which actually mean plot-value rises *are* stopped then the new Stamp Duty substitute remains the same.

How will the new annual LVT be paid?

Stamp Duty is a national tax, so it would be reasonable to continue this and make use of the usual income tax arrangement. LVT might mean no more than an adjustment in PAYE allowances.[1] In this way, the payment of the LVT is just another deduction in the monthly tax bill. Voters are far more aware of, and likely to complain about, any big one-off tax demand. It is good politics to have taxes paid as a small steady amount.

So, the long journey to stabilising the price of house can start. Then some of the asset that is the land under the house can be removed from the vagaries of mortgage lending and become a source of benign tax revenue which encourages enterprise and does not penalise and dampen enterprise a feature that income tax is believed to do. Housebuilders, freed from the burden of land-speculation, can then begin to build better houses and critically, many more of them. Owners of old properties can see the benefit of using their land to improve their housing condition. Replacing an old heat-leaking home with something better, with more useable space, with modern facilities becomes an attractive option. Memories of the broken housing market at the start of the twenty-first century will soon fade away.

---

[1] This idea was suggested to me by Tony Vickers of ALTER

The most difficult part of the journey is the first step. Let's do what it takes to stop rising house prices!

Chapter 16

Conclusion

There are <u>three</u> options for holding down house prices:

- Strictly limit banks' ability to create unlimited amounts of mortgage money. Ordering the banks to act prudently seems like a fools' errand. They will always find a way around Bank of England 'advice'. Hitting them where it hurts would be more effective. We could suggest that the Permanent Bank Levy could be ratcheted up by the same rate as house-price rises. This also offers the banks the chance to reduce their tax burden while virtue signalling but only if they manage to push down house prices. The practicalities of this are simple — an announcement in the next Budget would suffice.
- Nationalising all land used for houses, both new and that on which existing houses stand. Although there is the brilliant example of Singapore to emulate, openly stating this is unlikely to be a vote winner. Instead, some half-way stages could be implemented:
    - community land trusts be encouraged fiscally and through planning regulations
    - existing publicly owned housing could become 'government leasehold'. This would apply to right-to-buy from local authorities

- publicly owned land could be sold for development with the proviso that it remains under the same government leasehold system

It is not obvious that the UK government as a ground-landlord would act in the same benign way the Singapore or Hong Kong governments do to resolve the broken housing market. Conventional leaseholds are usually for a fixed and long-term, sometimes up to 99 years. This would not be the dynamic instrument to recover community-created value in land that we seek here, *unless* a very enlightened government chooses to make it so. Until such an arrangement reaches a very wide scale, it won't have much effect on the housing market.

- Extract the community-created wealth in the plot-value via a plot value charge. Enough has been said already that however desirable a uniform nationwide scheme of PVC might be, it must be approached slowly and carefully. Millions of existing homeowners would be horrified if their most significant asset was to be wiped out in the short-term and would vote accordingly. Longer-term, however, PVC will work directly on removing the land-value asset from the house price, thus eliminating the collateral that have allowed banks to vastly increase their mortgage lending. PVC works directly on the element of 'house price' which is the basis of the broken housing market.

As to which of these three is best and should therefore be promoted and encouraged, there is no straightforward or simple answer. What we can say with certainty is that the current situation is so desperate that maybe there's a need for all three to be promoted and tried. However, in the longer term, a dynamic form of plot-value charge would appear to us to be preferable.

Which house-prices should be stopped from rising?

Unfortunately, when economists talk of 'real' prices, they mean something imaginary. So much for the world of inflation-adjusted prices. 'Actual prices' are the amounts that you actually pay. When it comes to house-prices, comparisons are often usefully made with average earnings, and are a good indicator of affordability. So, when we say "Stop House Prices Rising" which of the prices are we talking about? There has been some ambiguity about this, but at the very least, the aim should be to stop prices rising faster than inflation generally.

Of course we would like to go further than just stopping inflation-adjusted prices from rising anymore. Stop inflation-adjusted prices falling matters too, especially in the short run. The grim period of the early 1990s, when 'negative equity' was experienced by many who discovered the amount they owed on their mortgage exceeded the fixed amount of their mortgage, is recalled by those affected as extremely worrying. If stabilising actual house prices became policy, it could lead to perverse effects if retail price inflation started up in earnest again.

Comparing house prices to average incomes would only be a long-term indicator. In reality it is the only indicator that matters. It is a crying shame that capitalism has failed to produce good quality homes in abundance at affordable prices. Commentators such as Liam Halligan (*ibid*) fear this failure might lead to the downfall of the system that has benefitted us in so many ways. We are well used to our high standard of living where food and clothing are available in abundance and where a cascade of wonderful consumer products are cheaply available. The broken housing market is a consequence of a latter-day version of financial capitalism. Lending institutions must gradually be weaned off the easy pickings from asset-based plot-value lending.

The first step is for the government to do what's really required to Stop House Prices Rising.

The urgency of doing so has never been greater.

References and further reading

Read what academics and journalists say about the Broken Housing Market. Some feel Inhibited from clean-cut policy proposals. There is a need to explain, but not solve the problem. ('Point and Sigh' is one description of this). But these academics have credibility, and importantly have done the research.

Bentley, Daniel (Nov 2017) *The Land Question: Fixing the dysfunction at the root of the housing crisis* Civitas—Institute for the Study of Civil Society Tufton Street, London SW1P 3QL and it's free to download too! Well worth a read. http://civitas.org.uk/publications/the-land-question/

Michael Ball (1988) Rebuilding Construction

Bolster, Anne (2011) Evaluating the impact of stamp duty land tax of first time buyer's relief *HMRC Working Paper 13* London —a gem of a paper!

Christophers, Brett (2018) *The new enclosure: The appropriation of public land in neoliberal Britain* London, Verso —'not very interesting; Marxism' says my revue, but important

Dorling, Danny (2015) *All that is Solid: How the Great Housing Disaster Defines our times , and what to do about it* UK Penguin —a great deal of 'point and sigh'

Galbraith, John Kenneth (1987) *A History of Economics: The Past as the Present* Hamish Hamilton, London.

Halligan, Liam (2019) *Home Truths: The UK's chronic housing shortage - How it happened, why it matters and how to solve it* London, Biteback —a brilliant book well worth reading, even if we don't agree with all of his conclusions

Harrison, Fred (2005 1st ed) *Boom Bust: House Prices, Banking and the Depression of 2010* Shepheard-Walwyn —the title says all you need to know about the impressive insight of this writer

Jerry Jones (2012) How a land value tax would help resolve Britain's housing crisis At http://www.labourland.org/downloads/papers/HousingCrisisPaper.pdf

Jones C. et al, (2018). An assessment of historic attempts to capture land value uplift in the UK, The Urban Institute, Heriot-Watt University —pdf (Commissioned by Scottish Govt)(very good details, also international comparisons)

Jones, Jerry and Carol Wilcox (2015 May) *A Strategy for replacing council tax and business rates with a land value tax: A first step towards a more equitable tax system* Labour Land Campaign.

Klein, Naomi (2007) *The Shock Doctrine: The Rise of Disaster Capitalism* London Penguin

Monbiot, George (ed) (2019 June) *Land for the many : Changing the way our fundamental asset is used, owned and governed* London Labour Party

Purves, Andrew (2015) *No Debt, High Growth, Low Tax: Hong Kong's Economic Miracle Explained* London: Shepheard-Walwyn

Ryan-Collins, Josh (2019) *Why Can't you afford a home?* Cambridge, UK Polity —the shorter and more accessible version of the next item.

Ryan-Collins, Josh; Toby Lloyd & Laurie MacFarlane (2017) *Re-thinking the economics of Land and Housing* London Zed/NEF —excellent, up-to-date, aware of wider issues

Timperley, Chloe (2020) *Generation Rent Why you can't buy a home (or even rent a good one)* Kingston-upon-Thames UK Canbury Press —a wonderful description based on first-hand experiences; highly recommended.

Wilcox, Carol (2018 Aug) *Fix the housing crisis by booting out the rentiers* Morning Star

Why not sign up to our mailing list here:

Why not browse our BOOKSHOP?

More about Bite-Sized Books here:

Made in the USA
Coppell, TX
23 March 2026

74451108R00066